THE DOOR IS A JAR - BILL HICKS

(excerpted from Mindful Artfulness)

Then Jesus went into the temple courts and drove out all who were buying and selling there. He overturned the tables of the money-changers and the seats of those selling doves. And He declared to them, "It is written: 'My house will be called a house of prayer. But you are making it into a den of thieves.'"

—Matthew 21:13

CONTENTS

Dedication

To David, Susie and Scout
with thanks, and appreciation
of your great talents

INTRODUCTION

"One time me and three friends dropped acid, drove round in my dad's car. He's got one of those talking cars. We're tripping. The car goes, "The door is ajar." We pulled over and thought about that for twelve hours.

'How can the door be a jar?'
'Shit, I don't know, but I see it.'
'I see it too.'
"Shit, I don't know. What's that?' Why would they put a jar on a car?'" [1]

—Bill Hicks, REVELATIONS, London,
Dominion Theatre, 1992

Welcome to the wonderful world of Bill Hicks.

Such a simple pun, Malapropism, and purposeful illusion of seeing one thing as another, when in reality ... or ... did it *really go down that way*?!

At one time in his all too brief life he tagged himself "Shiva the Destroyer of Comedy." Of course Bill had other liaisons as well. He was one of the original *Texas Outlaws* — a band of comedians. Sam Kinison was another one. Bill sings about this time of his life in a rare interview now unearthed and viewable on *Bill Hicks—The Complete Collection.*

There once was this group of guys
Gleam of madness in their eyes
Wanted to make their mark on the world
Outlaws was their name and,
Comedy was their game
Along with trying to meet some girls [2]

---

[1] See: *Love all the People*, p. 62. Bill Hicks routine recorded at The Funny Bone in Pittsburg, PA. 20 June 1991.

[2] See: *The OUTLAWS*, written & sung poolside by Bill Hicks, Houston, Texas, July 17, 1988.

When approaching Bill's life-long friend, photographer David Johndrow about the licensing rights to one photo (of thousands) he shot of Bill, I felt a great compliment that I'd gotten my inspection of Bill Hicks right. Because, Mr. Johndrow joined up to this small literary effort by allowing the use of his work. The photo you see is one of the last professional shots taken by his close friend. It is as detailed and perfect as the artist shooting wanted it to be. The subject surely approving his dear friend's razor-sharp instincts.

The Earth cries: "Oh Bill...we need you now...we really do."

The publisher agrees with me that this chapter from my 2017 volume *Mindful Artfulness* was a candidate for stand alone publication because we think the world not only enjoys Bill Hicks, but, the Earth needs what his spirit can conjure. When limitations confront a person, that is precisely the time to seek boundary-crossing entertainment (defined as anything that opposes negativism). Then it is time to jettison your mind away from evil divisive voices. As you will read, Bill Hicks had a prescription for this dilemma. You'll enjoy it.

GET YOUR HICKS ON

The clear thinking that Bill Hicks applied to the first Gulf War, *"Tommy — pull up G-12"* (from *Relentless)* is exactly the gut-level humor we can now apply to George H. W. Bush's son known as "W." He, "W" kept the party line and continued the Bush family history (war profiteering); proving that whenever someone named Bush gets into the Oval Office, they start something with Iraq. Bill's spot on imitation of Bush Sr.'s voice endears one to Bill if only that his mimicry skills are second to none.

The insipidness of the United States attacking a country (Iraq) that did nothing to the homeland (US), and having the Secretary of State (General Colin Powell), lie his ass off in front of the world at the United Nations about Saddam's "weapons of mass destruction" (which, by the way, were *never* found) — clearly shows us the bedrock of Hicks' cry, "All governments are lying cock suckers."

When meeting one of Bill's friends and trying to figure each other out, I think a lot was cleared away when I said, "Well, he predicted this world—2016—didn't he?" Another Bush. Another Middle-Eastern conflagration. The many Senators and Congressmen ousted from office for sexting teens from the Congressional gym (remember Representative "Carlos Danger"?) or another Congressman trying to score head in the Congressional men's room? There's nothing wrong with having sexual urges. There's everything wrong with Senators and Congressman making laws against gay men and women, when those Congressmen and Senators *are* in fact, gay! The hypocrisy is so thick it might take one of those Bradley tanks that was used to kill women and children at the Branch Davidian compound in Waco, TX, to cut through it. Bill Hicks and I take exception to the indiscriminate incineration of innocent children. The US government murdered twenty-seven people in America in cold blood because they did not conform to behavior others condoned as "normal." [3]

What would Bill have made of the Arizona Congresswoman shaking her constituents' hands in a mall in Arizona where a man drew a gun, and shot Representative Giffords in the head? Paralytic, and disfigured forever, she still lives to do her job. Unfortunately her fellow congressional civil servants did not do their jobs. The proliferation of guns under the pretense of the Second Amendment to the Constitution of the United States, still rages. The Amendment is used to defend gun ownership widely.

---

[3] In 1993 more than twenty children were burned to death in a fire Hicks showed banned videotape of in his final stage appearances. It showed that the fire was started by the ATF, a US government military force. The mass media did not show the footage—now widely known—showing that the Davidians did not set their compound ablaze. Not one single child ever testified to being sexually molested. In 1995, I toured the charred remains of the Waco site. The simple tent pegs with Polaroid pictures of the slain children, placed as "grave markers" made me physically ill, as did the rickety shack "museum" on the premises. The whole thing was so sad and unnecessary.

But the law states very specific patronage of gun ownership to "militias."

Bill addressed this. He said in England no one had any guns, even the cops! In 1991, he noted there were only fourteen deaths from handguns in all of England. Yet, in the US where handguns were plentiful, there were twenty-eight thousand deaths. But, he concluded, *"There is no evidence to suggest that there is any relationship between NOT having a gun and no handgun deaths; and having guns and many people getting killed by guns. And you'd be a fool and a Communist to think so."* Through counterpoint and the blatant skewering of hypocrisy he made audiences howl. And we are still howling. His spoonful of sugar was logic. He sometimes made this point by standing in arabesque position and playfully stating, "It's called logic. It'll help ya."

Anita Hill and her inappropriate pursuit by Judge Clarence Thomas after he watched some skin flick 80's style seems so tame now. Pee-Wee Herman getting caught in a porn theatre masturbating (what else are you supposed to do in there?) all seems so tepid given gas attacks that kill thousands in planned genocides across the globe. 9/11? A horrible nightmarish game-changer that I am glad Bill did not live to see. The 21st century began on that day letting us all know our technology and politicians cannot save us from evil.

Bill made us all laugh when he imitated Saddam Hussein having a gut laugh when George H. W. Bush was voted out of office after the Persian Gulf War. Bush's replacement? The sax-playing, hound dog Arkansas Governor Bill Clinton. It is almost as if a Hicks joke came to life! The President's seed on a blue spangly dress, kept by the "other" woman, sequestered by the FBI, impeached and then...Clinton's resurrection! Some of Bill's routines almost read as prescient hieroglyphics predicting what Shakespeare offered, "Past is Prologue." (You bet—and we never even mentioned Clinton's wife Hillary who became the Presidential nominee of her party, opposing...a misogynist madman who won!)

Hicks would have loved the controversy over Monica Lewinsky and that horribly stained blue dress. "Blow job gone wrong!

Film at Eleven!" How we wish we could have known what Bill would have said! (Cynical Hicks fans answer that Dennis Leary probably said it because Hicks fans know Leary lifted large portions of Hicks' material and none of us are happy about that.) Leary's "homage" and "like mindedness" is mule excrement. Pilfering isn't "paying tribute." It's thievery, period. Cynthia True shows this line-by-line in her celebrated 2002 biography, *AMERICAN SCREAM—The Bill Hicks Story.*

What would Bill have made of Bush's son (named George) coming back and whacking the Iraqi dictator one more time? (Ever thought of Bush 41 and Bush 43 as the Corleone family? Papa knocked out of power by an aggressive adversary, brings the son—Michael—to kill every threatening enemy. Life imitating art?)

Ask yourself, how many innocent Iraqi children were murdered because a son (George W. Bush) wanted to avenge an assassination attempt on his father's (George H. W. Bush) life? Now, Hicks challenges us all to answer that question. Do you have the guts? The interest? Do you care that the pinpointed attacks by ISIS in Paris, Turkey, Manchester (England), and Ft. Hood (US), all stem from blood on George W. Bush's and VP Dick Cheney's Swiss bank manicured hands?

Death finally came to Saddam as he faced his own people while awaiting the gallows. He was jabbed with sharp sticks as he took one step, his throat closed as his spine was snapped.

What would Bill have brought out of those gallows? Would he have made clever reference to the magical Mandrake plant that only grows beneath a hanged body seeded by the blood and semen ejaculated by the swinging corpse, in the light of the full moon? A nightshade toxic plant thought miraculous since prehistoric man. Also, the Mandrake encouraged "rutting"— making love. The Mandrake is an aphrodisiac! It is a fantasia of Hicksian interests. Had Bill only lived to see it!

There is one writer who emphatically states that Bill Hicks is the modern counterpart to the great writer and poet, Jonathan Swift (1667—1745). The mantle passed from Swift to Hicks, the author believes, and notes Hicks' use of words, sounds, and rhythmic elocution gallantly brought to the stage what, another great wordsmith, Bruce Springsteen, called "the whole package."

We'll never know, but his genius pushes us to think critically, seek the detailed truth; and rebel against (among others) the illusion of network news, and general media. An example:

> In 1986 *The New York Post* reported loudly on the front page: HITLER'S DIARIES FOUND! The very next day the same newspaper equally shouted on page one: HITLER'S DIARIES HOAX. It was never about the "truth." It was about selling papers to gullible commoners who are shoveled lies indiscriminately by lesser types who don't care what havoc they reap. Can't you just hear the Murdochian voices of black teeth-baring billionaires amidst a cloud of blue smoke saying coldly in some steely conference room, *"OK, Day One, let's give those assholes something about Hitler...what? Hmmmn. I know, let's say his diaries or some shit was found. Yeah, do that. And then, right, next day, we'll fuck'em up some more. Keep those masses docile and ignorant. Yeah, do that."*

How far are we from the truth by offering this? Well, given that publishing baron Rupert Murdoch's empire was tainted[4] to the level of him having to close the newspaper that hacked many people's (including her majesty Queen Elizabeth) cell phones to obtain so-called private information, I'd say the thrown knife has hit the center of the target.

---

4 See: Cowell, Alan, Somaiya, Ravi, *The Times of London Sued in Hacking Scandal — No End in Sight*, The New York Times, April 12, 2012.

THE DEN OF THIEVES

You can replace anything Bill Hicks has to say about the Kennedy assassination and plug in a more modern reference. Yes, the media, networks, and the politicians are all lying to us— anyone awake knows this. Would Bill Hicks have loved the revelation that all newscasters in the US are tele-prompted to say *exactly the same words*, as shown by Internet compilations? Bill knew Big Brother and died while trying to introduce us all to Orwell's powerful metaphor that wears deceitful sheep's clothing on the network evening news. Anyone remember NBC's Brian Williams who wantonly broadcast that he "bugged out of Fallujah — in Iraq — with the US 'lead command' at the time of the Iraqi build up..." At the time Williams was discussing, a tale three years old, he was kicking it in some Caribbean resort nowhere near bugging out with anyone...

And, just to make a happy little triad with Rupert Murdoch and Brian Williams, let's not forget that chap over at the esteemed *New York Times*. A lad named Jayson Blair decided to test the mettle of the century-and-a-half-old newspaper in 2003. *The Times'* self-discovery of this charlatan is nailed squarely in *The Times* own headline, *Times Reporter Who Resigned Leaves Long Trail of Deception*. Publisher Arthur Ochs Sulzberger Jr. called the revelations "A huge black eye. It's an abrogation of the trust between the newspaper and its readers."[5]

And these are the well-balanced voices of the free press?

Bill reminds us that un-checked freedom is anarchy. But at least we should call it for what it is: Rupert Murdoch, Brian Williams and Jayson Blair are rapacious liars and corporate hustlers who milked huge cash out of established, venerable oracles of freedom (ergo the free press), network news, and given these factual examples, probably details equally egregious yet unknown.

---

[5] See: *New York Times: Reporter Routinely Faked Articles* (Probe alleges made-up quotes, plagiarism in at least 36 stories), CNN.com, May 11, 2003.

When privacy is no longer a right, having deteriorated to becoming a "privilege" for those who can afford it, we are in the world of live video cameras smaller than match heads that record our most private bodily moments. (Ever hear of "pee cams"?) Don't believe me? Take a ride on that new fangled thing called the Internet. You'll marvel at what you previously did not know about the person drinking coffee across from you.

2017 is a world of veritably no rules used and abused by warring factions among us.[6] The strife by all the government rule-makers is that, as Bill deftly pointed out in the 1980's, was that their work, thoughts and actions are "no longer relevant."

Yet in 2017 the US has had a black ("African American") US President. Marijuana is legal in over twenty-six states. ("You wanna fix that deficit, then legalize marijuana" screamed Bill in 1986.) And, Hicks favorite past time, "por-nah-graphy," is now so widespread that sexually aware ten-year-olds arrive at the dinner table talking about lesbians, LGBT school mates, and why Sally didn't like Bobby asking for a blow job under the bleachers.

Bill wrapped all of this up so elegantly by shouting to audiences in city after city, "They're lying to you!" The book *What Would Bill Hicks Say?* is a welcome addition to critical thinking inspired by Bill pointed toward modern conundrums. These include: flagrant ignorance, ineptitude, sinecures, sycophants and environmental recklessness. Such as, folks who drill for oil in Oklahoma, so repeatedly, that earthquakes result! Most in Oklahoma government respond, "Well, we don't have enough data to make an informed decision." It boggles the mind that the world Hicks predicted is here. Has it always been so? Or, has our collective *un*conscious entered our collective conscious? Let's hope so.

---

[6] Yet, to also show light amidst the darkness Bill and I allude to; consider this. The same technology referred to as "pee cams" above also provided the ability for this writer use my iPhone to shoot, edit and title with graphics a sixty-second video of my doing magic in a hospital waiting room. Minutes after shooting my live performance in New York, a cancer patient in South Carolina saw this video I sent to him, and his pain was less that day, he told me

Bill was an amazing synthesizer. Only in death do we know that he could spot a comic jewel made by another (a close friend), and then honestly state, "tonight, that goes in the act." His humor makes one think with clarity. That is his great gift. This is art.

Maybe Osama Bin Laden was more Bill's cup of insane and rancorous brew? A man, formerly trained by the CIA to aid the Mujahedeen's fight against the marauding Russian army crossing the Afghanistan border to, *suddenly* (!) became capable of perpetrating such evil as the snatching of four commercial air flights to invoke havoc emotionally, financially, and spiritually all over the Earth? *Three-thousand plus dead*—sure, all in a day's work for Bin Laden and suicide flyers. This is reality, not a comic parody?

I can hear Hicks' almost falsetto laugh while lamenting the weasels mentioned above. Can his boundary-pushing "Goatboy" be so far away from the President of the United States (Bush 43) mentioning "rape rooms" and "cattle prod torture of young women" in his State of the Union Address (2002)? [7]

Any of those mentioned (Bush, Saddam, Osama, Clinton) would have become targets for the outlaw comic. For Hicks' targets was not the small stuff. He defined the famous statement that a "man's reach should exceed his grasp." Nothing defines that better than two aspects of Bill's life when he was diagnosed with cancer from the liver that spread to his pancreas in the final eight months of his life. He recorded two full comedy albums in the studio and in front of live audiences. In his final fourteen days upon this planet, he went dark. Radio silence. He did not speak. He embraced life without speech as he felt that the circle would be complete. He came from silence, he would return to silence.

Absolute s i l e n . . .

---

[7] In Goatboy's defense, however, we might mention he was a lover; not a fighter. We refer to the graphic similarity.

I'm a stalwart Hicks fan. I've devoured many of the hundreds of hours of his live appearances, albums, TV specials and writing. But, I am not a fan of his performance only. I admire his craft and his showmanship. He had true guts. Bill Hicks is a genuine hero. In the essay that follows you'll understand this further.

Cigarettes were to Hicks as cocaine was to Sherlock Holmes. Legal. Lethal. The obsession of addiction that fueled his Dr. Jeykll and Mr. Hyde. Bill's comedy was sometimes the "shadow self" of the voracious reader he was. Bill transformed Steinbeck's classic *The Grapes of Wrath* into an interstellar Joad family of tourist aliens. Cosmically funny?

The Hicks universe is always expanding. His theatrical density can only be appreciated by repeat listening and viewing. His collected writings show the fulcrum of his thinking. He began his *One Night Stand* TV special for HBO with a voice over of his thoughts, prior to walking on stage, "Dear Lord, thank you, tonight the message will be heard. Amen."

We do not see the private Bill Hicks on stage. In his stage performances, if you really study the man, you begin to feel not only his careful writing (once he commented "that was the best goddamn pun you will ever hear!"), but you may begin to see glimpses of the smiling, indeed, *shy* man. You may glimpse the innocent, self-educated seeker. Decoding his material (for influences and references) is only possible after you wipe the tears of laughter from your eyes when you watch this deft, graceful clown repeatedly.

Johnny Carson (1925—2005) was similarly shy. While this writer only spent twenty-minutes with the King of Latenight privately in his dressing room while he had his make up applied, I learned that was nineteen-minutes longer than the average bear got with Mr. C. I bring up Johnny Carson because both Bill and I worshipped the man. Others more knowledgeable about the real man Johnny Carson was told me I'd done something very unexpected and wholly unusual at a young age. I explained that Carson and I talked about magic. Now as a man of fifty-six I realize Carson saw himself in me at age fourteen. This was the time when *he* was about to develop his magician-alter ego, The

Great Carsoni. Make no mistake; Johnny Carson was a *great* magician.

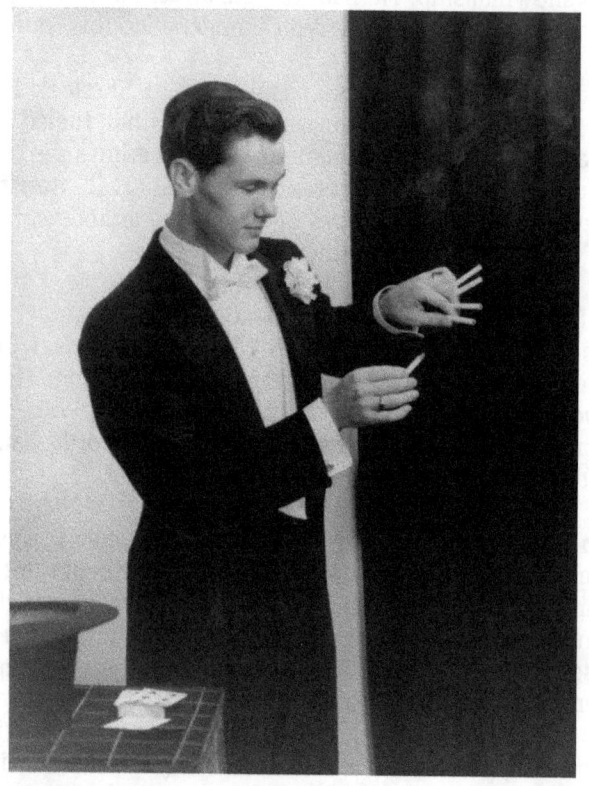

Johnny Carson, 1942, age seventeen before entering the US NAVY. Arguably the most famous and successful entertainer who ever graced television, he began as a magician named The Great Carsoni. Bill Hicks idolized Carson and studied him, right down to his cigarettes. Photo courtesy of: (Lincoln) Nebraska Photo Archives. Photographer unknown.

My detour to Johnny Carson is germane to this excerpted chapter from my book *Mindful Artfulness*. The notion is that both Carson and Hicks were great craftsman who knew that every breath, pause, cadence, move and "bookend" (the use of a repeating element at the beginning and end of a routine), was what made comedy performance great. The sad difference is that at the end of hosting *The Tonight Show Starring Johnny Carson* in 1992 after thirty years, Carson said with pride, "I did it." He was referring to having hosted the famous juggernaut late night *Tonight Show* from October 1, 1962 to May 22, 1992. Hicks was just starting on a Carson-like career (yet distinctly by his own mandates) when cancer cut him down, as his mother Mary stated at, "Thirty-two years, two months and ten days." (Bill was signed to do his own TV show, along with comic pal Fallon Woodland, in England on the BBC in his final year. *The Counts of the Netherworld* never came to be, as he passed during the very early stages of pre-production.)

Of course comedy is subjective. Different things make different people laugh. But, where Carson and Hicks meet on an even playing field is in their passionate rudder. You'll learn more about Bill's rudder in the essay that follows.

I've sharpened a few points, enlarged a few thoughts, corrected a few typos and offer an updated bibliography for the serious seeker. We've even solicited the work of Sheffield, England photographer Chris Saunders to make sure Bill was seen in England, because he became a star there. Bill joins those he praised who also passed young: Jimi Hendrix, Jim Morrison, Janis Joplin, and the Stones' drummer Keith Moon and The Who's drummer John Bonham.

We believe that Bill Hicks is needed now more than ever the way the Marx Brothers and other great comedians are being hailed by networks and marketers.[8]

---

[8] On Friday, May 19, 2017, in prime time, CBS-TV, aired the *I Love Lucy* program from the 50's starring Lucille Ball, her husband Desi Arnaz and special guest star Harpo Marx. The episode had been colorized and the estimated audience according to Nielsen Soundscan was 2.1 million people tuned in to see Lucy and Harpo's grand performance. The show was taped May 9, 1955, and featured Harpo's son Bill's arrangement of *Take Me Out to the Ball Game* played by Harpo on his harp. Somebody in network TV land is surely sending in the clowns. The good clowns.

LOVE ALL THE PEOPLE

Earth is approaching an abyss of nuclear proliferation that is unprecedented if the so-called people in power have their way to make this one world with one ruler. *"Shearing the herd"* is a phrase used by sub-basements analysts at the CIA when discussing the solution to population explosion. (In 2017, there are nine billion humans on Earth.) Yet, note the stark contrast of Bill's life's writing released as "Love All the People" showing the best tenets of his Christian appreciation. Rather than make things better for "all people" and taking that as the base line of action; Hicks spotlighted a gruff, idiosyncratic, imaginary military field commander ordering, *"I don't want any gay guys around me when I'm killin' kids. Just can't have it!"*

Resist bad hair day politicos' totalitarianism with every fiber of your body. Listen to Hicks and think for yourself. Wipe away that detritus of glossy magazine fodder, soap opera morals and ethics. Avoid the general dumbing down of popular culture. Turn off the TV. Read a book. Use your mind. Really radical stuff, I know.

Tell the truth and serve your fellow humans with the compassion that is inherent in us all. When truth is pointed out, it can be scathingly funny. "Get your Hicks on!" doesn't mean to worship Bill necessarily. It means to remember not to be swayed by anything less than you desire, or feel comfortable with. Independence and compassion are the values worth thinking about at the basis of Bill Hicks' self-described "editorializing." And just so you know, when asked earlier in his career what his "point" was, he replied, "Good entertainment."[9]

Bill Hicks, in life, and now in death, has been a true leader to many around the world. He is in fact a sane man. Ten years after his death, he was included in the daily record of Parliament.

---

[9] See: Youtube.com "Bill Hicks Rare Interview from 1988."

Modern biographers[10] place Bill Hicks alongside two of his heroes, Mark Twain and W.C. Fields. What drove this man of many talents awaits you!

Bill's message is simple: never let go of freedom of speech, mind, thought, spirit and action. Let the artfulness of your own life be your defiant statement to resist those who make laws based on evil divisiveness. Do not follow the television eye, mind and dictum; the products pushing commercial TV are a distraction from truer satisfactions. Let Bill Hicks bring those satisfactions front and center with great wit. Hicks hilarity is a sphere; not a circle. There is more here than meets the eye and ear immediately. The following ten-thousand-word essay will introduce some to Bill, hopefully titillate fellow fans, and possibly warm FOB's — our only desire.

Bill Hicks' body may have left Earth in 1994, but, his spirit, body of work and legacy lives. Like his hero Chaplin discovering his re-entry visa to the US was only granted for ten days in 1972, Chaplin mentioned to his wife Oona, "They're still afraid of me." I think Chaplin took some satisfaction in that, despite the accolades, awards and feting Lincoln Center gave him first on his triumphant return to the country that forced his exile.

Similarly, without mentioning the miscreants involved in corrupting Bill's legacy, it can be reported that: while his body has vanished, his Great Will lives. (That is not an empty hope. No, in humor that approaches how good Bill Hicks was, you feel "him." I believe, yes, the infamous "they" are afraid of him too. But do "they" know whom "he" actually lives in? Better call the Ghostbusters.)

Is truth threatening? Yes. Composer-sound designer Mark Bennett (*Out Of Order*, *The Coast of Utopia* among others) told me recently, "Reality is under attack." I agree. Truth indeed *does* threaten the "reality-changers." False news? Well, it has always

---

10 See: Dorman, Lawrence, *The Dictionary of Snark* (2013). Hicks stands alongside Dorothy Parker, Robert Benchley, S. J. Perelman, Groucho, W.C. Fields, Mark Twain and others who confounded and entertained with timeless clarity.

been around in many other incarnations. When the good guys do this, it's called "Positive Propaganda." When the bad guys change social structure for the minority, attempting to control the masses with dis-information, then . . . oh, wait. Wrong meeting! That's the material for the meeting at the docks tonight (eye wink).

Of course, I'm quoting Bill. See? He's sylph-like; such a joy. So charming. Very clever. (The meeting begins at midnight at Pier 40 . . . *shhh.*)

Bill stated frequently, he wanted two things out of life: to be a rock star, and to do as adventurous things with comedy as Charlie Chaplin had done. A dozen albums and ten DVDs later (all but two CDs delivered posthumously), nearly twenty-five years after his bodily exit, Shiva the Destroyer of Comedy, never left. He influences world culture just as surely as there is evil to fight. You don't need to understand the cast of characters Bill talked about to "get Bill." Spotlighting ignorance, making broad exaggerations and aligning unexpected bedfellows should provide laughter.

In 2004, transcendental artist Alex Grey spoke at his Chapel of Sacred Mirrors during a meeting of psychedelic minds. In attendance were Gary Panter (set designer for *Pee-Wee's Playhouse*), Trey Parker (*South Park, Book of Mormon*) and the late Jon Dix (video visionary for Radiohead's 2003 world tour). Grey said, "While Terence McKenna, Bill Hicks and Tim Leary have all passed, by natural or nefarious means, thousands, if not millions have risen to heed their charge." Stand with us and gleefully open your eyes. The laughter will encompass your hunger for the truth, and you won't feel entirely powerless.

Lord Krishna tells the Kshatriya (a warrior caste) Arjuna (in *The Bhagavad-Gita*, 400 BC—479 AD some scholars argue) that there was never a time when they did not exist. Krishna goes on to explain that opposites continually commingle in this ever-changing cycle of "samsara" (or "ever-suffering"). Similarly, Bill Hicks is still here. His work exists to inspire others to hold the light (and spear) of accountability to greedy plunderers; take your pick, unfortunately there are many.

With his educated entertainment pointed at our collective consciousness, Bill is ready to rock and roll when you need him. Use this notion.

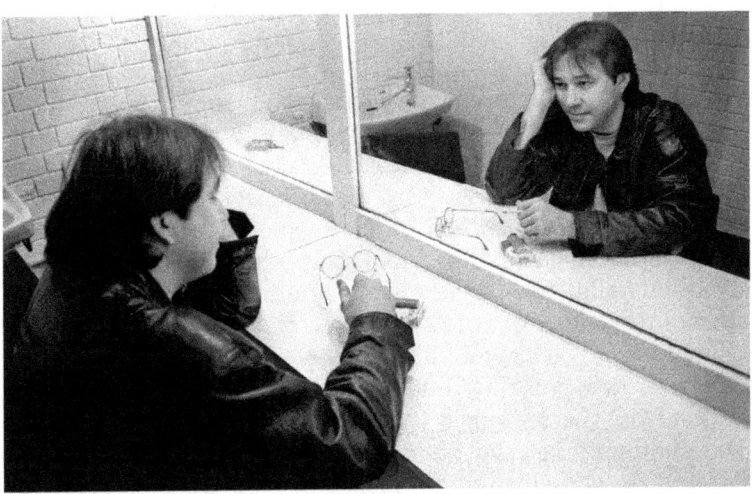

Bill Hicks seen backstage before going on at The Royal Northern College of Music *(Manchester/ UK), May 1992. Photo © 1992 Chris Saunders, Sheffield, England. All Rights Reserved. Used by permission. www.chrismsaunders.com*

Bill raised the bar to heights mere outrageousness doesn't come close to approaching. His words, actions, and output are not inconsequential, to use a proper double negative. He loved the bastardization of language wryly noting that if some people were titled, "Consulting Coordinators" then he was an "Amusement Engineer." Roaring laughter greeted that clear observation because we all know meaningless titles are inherently silly. And silly people sling silly titles. Then the knife: Bill's humor makes us notice that some people *kill* for titles. Some of those covetous title bearers Hicks slayed were religious zealots. Their word of God was theirs and theirs only!

Imitating Jimmy Falwell (1933—2007, a debauched, defrocked televangelist), Hicks shouted (imitating the preacher), *"I think what God meant to say was..."* Bill: "Gee? Hmmmn. I've never been that confident in my life. Rewrite God's sentiments!? That middleman thing is cute, it's wacky and I get it. But, the only god I pray to is in myself and its name is Love. Sorry, I gotta go, there's a voice a'callin' me."

Sure, he was just a foul-mouthed comedian. Sure . . .

The more people who hear Bill Hicks' comedic truths, the better off we ALL shall be. Because, we will have evolved to seeing clear solutions; as opposed to the people who repeat the same mistakes in the name of progress. *Seven* former Directors of the Central Intelligence Agency were briefing the new President-elect in November of 2016. The Directors all said essentially the same thing: "You cannot kill your way out of jihad." One of the Directors was reliably quoted saying: "The President-elect responded, 'Thanks. When I want your opinion, I'll ask for it.'" The same mistakes...over and over. Compassion can be learned through the truth that humor makes us feel, realize and act on. Killing in the name of peace is as ridiculous as attacking the wrong country.

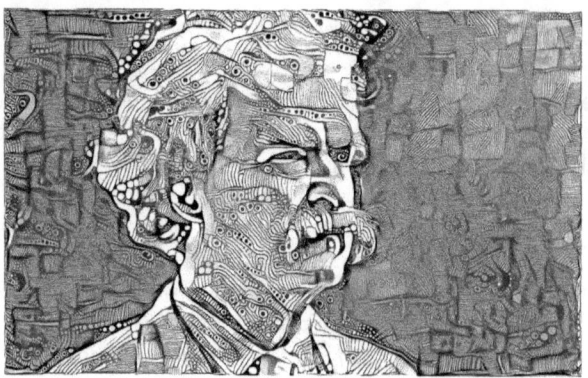

Bill Hicks admired Mark Twain very much, see pages 37-38.
Mark Twain photograph rendered through augmented intelligence
by Surreal Studio artist Duff Hendrickson, Seattle, WA, 2017.

Bill Hicks was not a saint. How could he be? He was a man. But I believe his fellow Outlaw Comic John Farnetti correctly stated, without puffery or false adulation to Bill in death, "In my mind, there is Bill Hicks" and then Mr. Farnetti made a sweeping gesture to show space between where he noted Hicks being, and then added with absolute certainty, "and then there's all the rest." I agree.

Bill Hicks reminds us:

We are one species sharing one consciousness with a greater cosmic mind.

Hicks' hilarity heals—undeniable.

He came, his message bold, keeps us laughing.
We are enlivened.

The spectacular comet Bill Hicks still illuminates our planet.
You are invited to stand in this effervescence.

Enjoy the mind-opening, deliriously funny ride.

"Welllll, it looks like we got ourselves a read-ah !"

—Ben Robinson
Chaplin Circle
New York, 2017

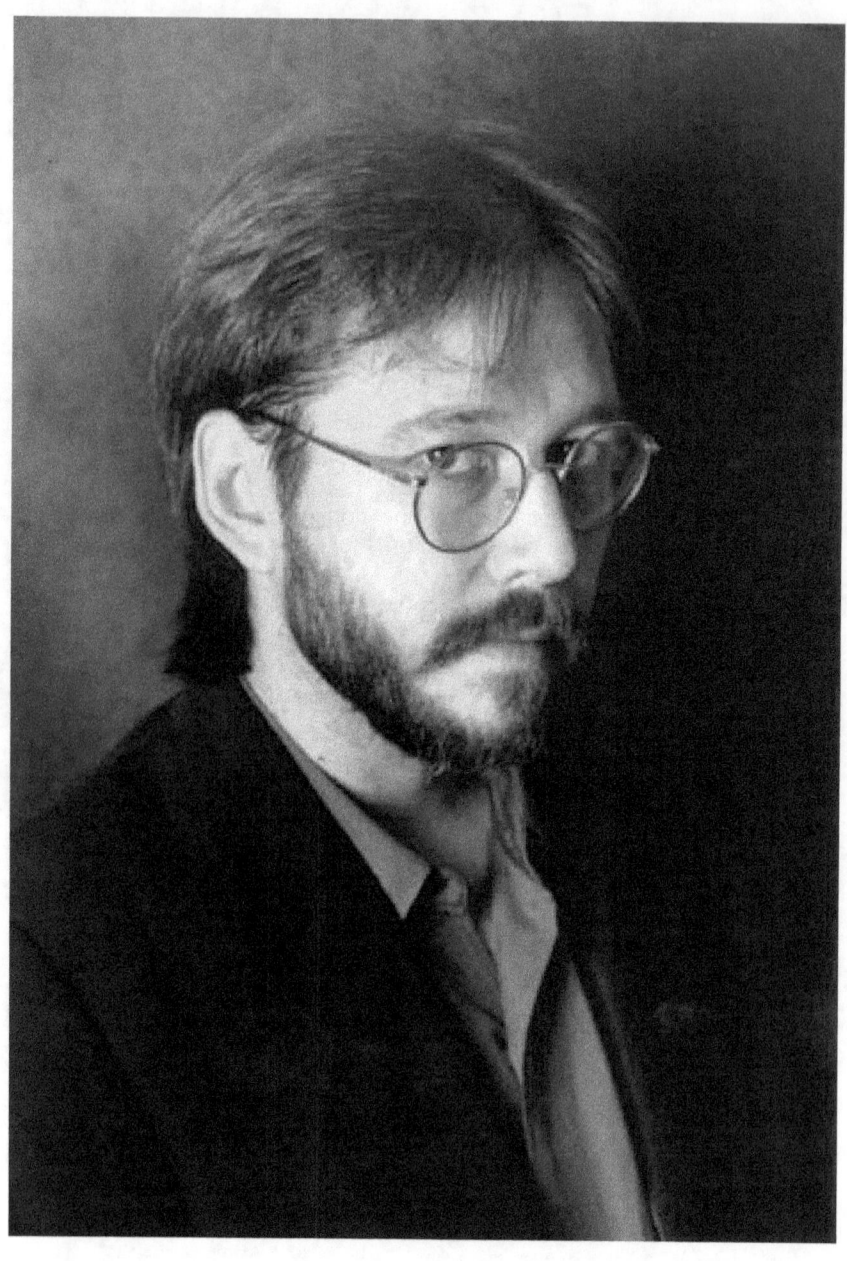

Bill Hicks in one of his final photo sessions with his longtime friend David Johndrow. Copyright © 1994 David Johndrow. All Rights Reserved.

BILL HICKS

Bill Hicks (1961—1994), died at age thirty-two. Here are thirty-two descriptions of him.

1. Musician
2. Comedian
3. Stand-up Philosopher
4. Experimenter
5. Writer
6. Dreamer
7. Social Critic
8. Dancer
9. Athlete
10. Devoted friend
11. Lover
12. Profanist
13. Brother
14. Boyfriend
15. Guitarist
16. Explorer
17. Spiritually-centered
18. Diarist
19. Recovered Alcoholic
20. Smoker
21. Bibliophile
22. Son
23. Long-distance driver
24. Satirist
25. Urban Shaman
26. Angry teen
27. Cancer-ridden
28. Genius
29. Erotica connoisseur
30. Trickster
31. Preacher-speaker
32. Poet

So it is that I begin this essay about this multi-talented individual who unfortunately confirms, "only the good die young." Hicks said of himself on his *Love, Laughter & Truth* CD, "I deal only in facts. That's why I am a cocky fucking bastard." Strap in—the ride coming is a *r i d e .*

I have an odd relationship with this man I never met. He was born exactly one year and one day after I was, as he says, "screaming in America." I was invited to a midnight show Hicks was doing in the late 1980's in New York City in Greenwich Village at the famed Village Gate on Bleecker Street. I declined to go because of an audition I had early the next morning. Not seeing him live is one of the very few regrets I have.

Any performer is much greater than a taped show. You cannot "feel" the performer, the way a live audience can. Between the audience and the performer is tension and drama in the room/hall that doesn't translate to the home viewing audience. This is because the representative medium (tape or DVD or Internet viewing) cannot capture the sights, sounds, smells or sweat of the comedy-viewing audience. In the early 21st century, the archetypal model of electronic and drug-induced virtual entertainment has challenged live entertainment.

There was nothing virtual about Bill Hicks. "Like any good artist, all of Bill's interests showed up in his work" wrote Jimmy Pineapple in tribute to his dear friend when Bill died.[11]

He was in your face, took control, and no prisoners — in the name of the *truth*. He shocked, inspired and pillaged sanctimony and hypocrisy. He made the point that marijuana was illegal because it was "one of those un-taxed drugs." Anyone who ever saw the comedian agrees, Bill Hicks changed the game. (It may *not have* been his goal to do this; he operated from instinctual understanding of his passion, goals and where he was on the path to attaining commercial success. But "more personal success" was rooted in a genuine path he sought to spiritual Enlightenment; cosmic awareness. By confronting the truth to the public on stage, he courted the juice of conflict and resolution to take himself *and his audience* on indeed one hell of a ride for the evolution of ideas and no-holds-barred consciousness expansion.)

---

[11] See: Booth, Kevin, *Bill Hicks: Agent of Evolution*, HarperCollinsBooks, UK, 2005, p. 417.

To state that he was a "rock'n roll comedian," as many journalists have described him, is fatuous at best. The description misses the point entirely, because it mentions his form, not his content. Bill Hicks would be the first to disagree with anyone putting him in any kind of box. Only *he* could put himself in whatever description fit, he felt.

No doubt, if you are turned off by profanity on the page or the stage, or in general, then a man who used a New Yorker's favorite word, every other sentence, might not be your cup of tea. (So if certain profane words offend you, or concepts that are seemingly radical upset you, turn the page.)

Hicks slayed as a comedian with what he termed "social criticism." He spoke on stage in the US, Australia, Canada and England (where he finally achieved proper recognition), with the truth as he saw it. In the UK he was called a "satirist." Whether it was President George H. W. Bush arming smaller countries, and then ordering attacks on those countries, or the War on (untaxed) Drugs, Hicks shone his light on the hypocrisy of the US government in all of its ugly, warring bravado.

"Because" as the comedian parodied the former President's voice, "we still live in a dangerous world." Hicks offered the button line, "Because of you, you fucker! Stop arming the world, man!" People gasped for air because they'd been socked in the comedic solar plexus. It was funny all right, and it made you think. Hicks' angst at the tales he told was palpable. You can imagine what happened when he called the ATF (Bureau of Alcohol, Tobacco and Firearms—a government military force) a "bunch of pussy cowards who burned people to death in their own homes. Nazi killers all, you fucks."[12] His self-description as a "misanthropic humanist" is eloquent and while accurate, touches on intellectualism he found "off-putting to bovine America."

He spoke of only two kinds of faith; that which is founded in love, or driven by fear. He spoke of God and railed at audiences at the *Just For Laffs* festival in Canada in 1991, "There is

---

[12] See: Bill Hicks at Igby's. His final performance, Los Angeles, CA, November, 1993.

nothing stronger than the Will of God. *N-O-T-H-I-N-G ! ! !*" At the same performance (titled "Relentless," viewable on DVD) he also spoke of playing musical instruments from the heart, as he was wont to do. (It is believed by many who knew him that Hicks was primarily a musician who did comedy. Not a comedian who dabbled in music.) Yet, to emphasize his point he argued, "If it is a difference between musicians dying while drowning in their own vomit, or New Kids on the Block, then I want my rock stars to play from their heart with a gun to their head and then say 'I hope you enjoyed the show!' " Then Hicks made a loud gun shot noise into the microphone, and it was as if the rock guitarist had shot himself. To which Hicks screamed "Yeah, *Y-e-a-h !!!*" while he jumped in the air with both legs bent backward. Hicks said, "If it is a question of good tunes or listening to the Devil's music...at least he fucking jams! I'll be hanging ten as I surf on the Lake of Fire high fiving Satan each time I pass him." Audiences were shocked and laughed. Pause ... maybe ten seconds. The sweat poured from his brow. The performance exhausted everyone present. Then he quietly said into the microphone, "I am available for children's parties."

Pandemonium.

The audience was withered and elated at the same time. They were indeed experiencing something new.

Only Hicks could set up a punch line of counterpoint between being "(also) available for children's parties" and previously screaming in joy and leaping high into the air because your favorite rock star had finished his set by killing himself with a gun. Only he could follow such considered insanity and take his audience to even further realms of his mind. As Kevin Booth titled his book about his best friend: Bill was an "agent of evolution." The book he wrote about his friend runs over four hundred and fifty pages.[13]

Usually after his forty-five minute set, in a US comedy club, or after an hour-plus performance in a UK theatre, he closed his

---

[13] See: Booth, Kevin (with Michael Bertin), *Bill Hicks: Agent of Evolution*, HarperCollinsEntertainment, UK, 2005.

shows toward the end of his young life with a message about taking all of the money governments spend on weapons and armaments, and, instead, feeding, clothing and educating the poor of the world, "not one human life excluded, and we can explore space, inner and outer, forever in — peace." Upon the mention of the word "peace" three gunshots rang out apparently killing the comedian. His point: unmistakable.

Apparently, the politicians he criticized didn't find him funny, nor think his "social criticism" (often cited as being in league with Lenny Bruce or Mort Sahl) was helpful to maintaining social order (as the government saw fit).[14] These politicians did not like "a foul-mouthed comedian" telling the masses to think for themselves (and not follow as blind sheep to what TV newscasters spewed). Bill Hicks was an original that has been copied in style possibly, but never in impact, timing or originality. Today he is widely accepted as "the greatest comedian of his generation."

It doesn't take comic style to enhance greatness; it requires a belief system that the believer finds unchallengeable. One word describes him in my opinion: fearless. He truly did not care if he was accepted. He cared about having something to say and saying it to the best of his ability. Like many great artists, what was personally inside him was amplified on stage as a theatrical rendition—and entertainment for others—that was more animated than the private man. Hicks was a seeker. Seen in hindsight, he was a genuine prophet (of sorts). He came, burned brightly for his Warhol fifteen and then split. His legend grows every time another learns of him. His life was perfect three-act drama: Boy prodigy, young seasoned professional, early death cementing his legend. Hicks' yin yang was part explosive young talent Elvis Aaron Presley and part surviving Tibetan monk run out of his homeland and speaking about the injustices of the world with logic, reason, compromise and compassion. (Bill actually saw The King in concert twice. And only Bill's

---

[14] Hicks' familiar rant concerning his interpretation of the US government's 1993 assassination of David Koresh's Branch Davidian compound in Waco, TX: "You are free to do as we tell you." Twenty-seven people were murdered in cold blood, including children. America yawned along with what else was on the TV evening news that night. Hicks' indignant scream only got louder.

summation of his appreciation of Elvis is accurate, *"Some played E in Vegas. I play E's last hour. Wuh!"* His impersonation of Elvis probably sent a few people to the Emergency Room they were laughing so hard.)

We are not concerned with gooey adulation necessarily, but inspection of Hicks' tortured genius and his light that burned so brightly, so quickly. Studying Hicks is like one of those dolls that you keep opening and opening and the more you open it, the more dolls you find. Let's call those "dolls" what Bill called them, "truth, love and laughter."

THE DEFINTION OF A ONE MAN SHOW

In a Hicks performance, such as his last TV special filmed at the two-thousand-seat Dominion Theatre in London's West End, he could play *all of* the following roles in a simple stage concert. [15]There, he truly delivered the definition of a one-man show that happened to include:

A woman receiving cunnilingus, a man receiving fellatio, a man trying to give himself fellatio, his mother, a State trouper, a hallucinating driver, a military general, field troops setting off bombs, a character named "Goatboy" who practiced sex between humans and animals, a shy little girl, a character cut out of a hit movie, Democrats, Republicans, the hero cowboy, a man driving a truck, a Waffle House waitress, rednecks, offended Fundamentalist Christians, Satan the Devil, God, Jesus Christ, moths flying to the sun, no talent musicians and pop stars, President John F. Kennedy being assassinated, dumb fat Americans, and finally—himself.

---

[15] The producer of that show explained that the show was attended by an extra four hundred people standing at the back packed against the back of hall, Hicks' talent, buzz and recognition commanded. Most of those people were "industry."

But that was not all; nor does this essay seek to note all of his attributes, historically or creatively. This is a smattering of a larger universe we invite you to explore. In the Hicks universe, one of Woody Allen's jokes pervades:

Interviewer: *Mr. Allen, is sex dirty?*
Woody Allen: *Only if done correctly.*

So, let the Hicks chariot away! Be damn sure, you bring no road map other than your interest; this is tricky terrain. Only the educated and brave survive. The Hicks Funhouse is childlike inquiry that provides insightful fun.

"I used to drink and do drugs.
About a year now I've been without it.
But I'd like to thank management for offering."
—Bill Hicks, 1989

His closest friends (Dwight Slade, Kevin Booth and David Johndrow) all enthusiastically chimed that Hicks was a very loyal friend who was an unstoppable force that met an unmovable object (the death of the American dream). Kevin Booth often stated that there was only one person who could "make me do some things, and that was Bill." Together they took drugs and had experiences only they know about. They remember his tolerance for excess whether it is women, sex, and drugs, driving four days straight near the end of his life. Or, while ingesting his first mixed alcoholic beverage; when he downed seven straight margaritas and then went on stage to deliver his comedy set. Alcohol and Bill seemed to create his Mr. Hyde before his joining Alcoholics Anonymous and became sober for the rest of his life.

Whatever he applied himself to, in poker terms, he was "all in." His presence, thunderous. His personal demeanor—deeply considered. He was a genuine artistic role model for the dearth of experience needed to ascend to such wonderful performance. Bill knew that one perfectly delivered gut busting funny line was often the result of many hours trying that line many different ways.

The vice of his life were cigarettes. He engaged his love and fear of the nicotine drug by stating, "I'm a heavy smoker. I go through about two lighters a day." Alcoholism had its consequences: he was fired from jobs; he wasn't funny. Irreverence was replaced by instability, a word used by those that were there at the time. But, when he got clean and sober, his mother noticed it immediately in his eyes. She said his eyes were "clearer." Mary Hicks said she accepted her son as he was at any time. She never called him on his excessive drinking—she said it was simply something he had to go through. Luckily, the disease did not kill him.

One repeating memory from many who knew him, particularly his older brother Steven, remember that if he were booked in a club and you saw him "throw away a line" (meaning not give it emphasis) in less than a minute, then all week at the same club, he'd work on that line. By the end of the week, he'd have another four-minute pearl of comedy because of his unrelenting style to fix, nurse, cajole and tease humor from the most truthful, if not embarrassing situations he satirically created on stage. The connections Hicks made between terminally ill elders and stunts in the movies are a surprise too good to spoil; so we encourage your presence at a Hicks show on DVD. Beware; immersing oneself in the Hicks milieu is a mind-expanding experience. Binge watching Hicks on Youtube.com has curative affects for those saddled with depression; proving Norman Cousins thesis that laughter can eradicate illness.

Contemplating and laughing at Bill Hicks is the breath of fresh air of freedom to think original thoughts. This is the expansive area of the Will where only the sturdy play. If there are Chiefs and Indians, Bill Hicks was (and continues to be) a Chief who inspired Indians to think for themselves. "Get your Hicks on" is one of my mantras. In other words, think clearly. If humor is rooted in truth, the surprise of honest observation and the guts to reveal such is what centered Bill's delivery (method). But more, he delivered comedy the way a shark pursues its quarry—with relentlessness. Like John Cazale, Hicks knew the act of asking questions that may not be answered was the first step to finding answers. This is the "follow" in "follow through." In other words, the act of pursuit itself can sometimes bring great reward. During Hicks' early years, he might have noticed that Woodward and Bernstein of *The Washington Post* laughed out loud every time the Nixon White House provided a "non-denial-denial." Such became the bare bones of hypocrisy pillaged by Hicks in his late twenties. His comic voice now focused: fuck the Dad impersonation when there were Presidents to hold accountable! (It should be noted that Hicks' imitation of his father was one of his very first runaway successes, he being booked on the strength of bringing the skewering of his parents to the stage.)

Bill Hicks was a comedy workman. He saw the craft of stand up comedy as an end in itself. He was not trying to use it to "get somewhere" as others' did to enter TV situation comedies, film or get endorsement deals. Hicks plainly said that if any talent chose to promote a product, no matter how small, or possessing quality, that the "talent" was "Forever banned as part of the artistic community. You don't make our roll call because you don't play for our team. You're not an artist. You're a capitalist sucker of Satan's cock. A cheap whore."[16]

Comedian/magician Harry Anderson once said, "You can't sell out if no one is buying." But Hicks believed in the sanctity of his words as truth that made people laugh. More importantly . . . think. I think Bill Hicks was aware on a level that is "challenging" if not daunting to the individual. Like the Marx Brothers, making a chaotic vaudeville in their now-celebrated film *Duck Soup* (1933) out of warring nations ("Freedonia vs. Sylvania"), Bill Hicks was ahead of his time showing the absurdity of a government covering up the assassination of a US President. [17]

Bill Hicks was a true art warrior. He was uncompromising, stubborn and staunch in his belief that what he was saying and doing was the only thing he was put on Earth to do. His mother Mary once held her thumb and forefinger not far apart and said to her son, "Bill, you are just this close to being a preacher." Hicks replied, "Mom, I am a preacher." After his tragically

---

[16] See: *Revelations*, and transcript of Hicks' penultimate Monday performance at Caroline's at the Seaport (New York, November, 1993.)

[17] President John F. Kennedy possibly brought the world near nuclear annihilation. He was assassinated November 22, 1963.

young death from pancreatic cancer in 1994, his mother stated, "What Bill talked about was timeless, because it was true. There is no shelf life to the truth. Truth is forever."

Mrs. Hicks was right. In 2017, nearly a quarter century after her son's death, there are five full books written about him: *American Scream, Bill Hicks: Agent of Evolution, Love All the People (the writings of Bill Hicks), What Would Bill Hicks Say?* and Paul Outhwaite's deeply insightful *One Consciousness: An Analysis of Bill Hicks' Comedy.*

He left behind four fully realized TV specials, a plethora of listening CD's (see discography at end), most released posthumously.

His cult hit short film titled *Ninja Bachelor Party* has a pulsing life of died hard fans that smile with pride when they announce it is "the only film Bill Hicks acted in, much less several roles." The Bill Hicks legacy was described by one insider as "thriving." And, if he is being quoted by his friend Kevin Booth correctly, of "wanting to do with comedy what Chaplin did" then it has taken a quarter century for his followers to educate themselves to what Bill knew. He could imitate anybody or anything, as Chaplin deftly demonstrates in his masterpiece LIMELIGHT when Chaplin's character Calvero shows Claire Bloom's character that he can imitate a piece of bamboo. Hicks' talent was metamorphic like the men he admired.

Hicks played a character named Dr. Death in his short film *Ninja Bachelor Party.* The voice was very similar to the one he used to portray Satan in later comedy performances. It is the decision by this artist to make a point that excites our imagination. NBP took nearly ten years to finish. It was an effort by friends to hang out, laugh hard and enjoy themselves. A thousand people filled the Austin Opera House when the film premiered and Bill said with a straight face introducing the film, "When my management brought me the property to consider for my involvement, I was pleased to discover the insightful depths in the script." One of the co-creators stated that the audience began laughing immediately once the picture rolled, but the collaborators did not know if they were enjoying the film or laughing at the creators' amateurish efforts. Today, anyone who knows this fringe film finds kinship in like-minded souls. It is a very funny movie.

A feature-length documentary has been made in England (running time: over two hours). A UK short-form documentary (titled in the US *It's Just a Ride*) was done to complement the release of his live recordings on DVD (after his death). The extras on the feature documentary (*American: The Bill Hicks Story*) offer more than five hours of material, including this personal, audio-recorded diary entry made when he moved to LA at age eighteen:

> *"Hello, this is Bill. I just needed to talk to somebody. This tape recorder is all I've got right now. I haven't been funny in a long time. I haven't come up with new material in a long time. And I'll tell you, there's nothing scarier than to have forsaken the college life, the easy life, coming out here. What if I am just not funny? I have nothing! I am a bum."*

Let it be known in the spirit of true artistry that so-called "big names" like Gene Hackman and Dustin Hoffman both admitted freely that after they finish a play, film or any project, they genuinely felt that they might never work again. This is the plight and condition of the artist. It was the condition—perhaps as is popularly stated—of Bill Hicks, as true an artist as the actors cited.

In pre-9/11 America each one nighter did not take three days as it does now, due to travel constraints. Consequently, even Robin Williams is shown in a documentary (on his life) driving between many comedy clubs in Los Angeles, saying, "The only way to do the life of a stand up is to do it...before it does you."[18]

Hicks was not content with the standard William Morris contract handling comedians fed into the national network of comedy clubs that amounted to a neat two-hundred and twenty nights a year on the road, playing clubs and living in cheap hotels. No,

---

[18] Robin Williams (1951—2014) committed suicide, like Hunter Thompson, not willing to live with debilitating disease. In 2016 The Robin Williams Center was opened by the Screen Actors Guild Foundation on West 54th Street in New York City.

his friends (Kevin Booth and David Johndrow) agree that he was an "all or nothing guy." John Lahr, the esteemed theatrical critic of *The New Yorker* who wrote a five-thousand word profile of Hicks (in 1993, published four months before Hicks' death[19]) stating that Hicks was playing "Something like two-hundred and eighty three nights on the road each year to refine his work. He'd take a (comedic) line that had potential, and craft it into a gem by the end of that week's engagement." Biographer Cynthia True's [20]statement that "Bill Hicks played every comedy club in the US" is probably accurate. From 1989 to 1992 he was a genuine road rat racking up close to three hundred performances a year! "The gig's free, we get paid to travel" many have said about such a grueling schedule. Inspiration carries one far.

Where did Bill Hicks' inspiration come from?

As a child he saw the first comedic film made of Ian Fleming's novel featuring James Bond: *Casino Royale* (1967). It was a wacky movie with Peter Sellers playing Evelyn Tremble (aka James Bond 007) and Woody Allen playing "Jimmie Bond." The movie was a parody of the Bond ethic, world, and mostly portrayed Bond as a character that could not ever be taken seriously. How wrong those producers turned out to be! But Woody Allen's performance was a revelation to young Hicks. He realized Woody Allen could stand on a stage and cast pearls over the audience, make a point, be loved and still looked like a kid that was bullied unfairly in science class in Fifth Grade because he looked odd to others. Woody was the smartest guy in the room. Hicks loved that. Hicks had a baby face that spit lethal acid.

The other influence was Charlie Chaplin (1889—1977).

The similarities between Chaplin and Hicks are few. But there is one extremely important and definite correlation that speaks to

---

[19] See: *The Goat Boy Rises* by John Lahr, The New Yorker, November 1, 1993.

[20] See: True, Cynthia, AMERICAN SCREAM: The Bill Hicks Story, Pan Books, London, 2002, p. 118.

each individual's mindful artfulness. Both became stars in another country. In fact, considering that Chaplin became a star in the US, and Hicks became a star in England—the irony is only worthy of history and the truthfulness each artist banked on. If Chaplin showed the grave injustices to "the little fellow" and battled back with intelligence, grace and brilliant abstraction; Hicks took names, kicked ass and didn't care. Both were hysterically funny.

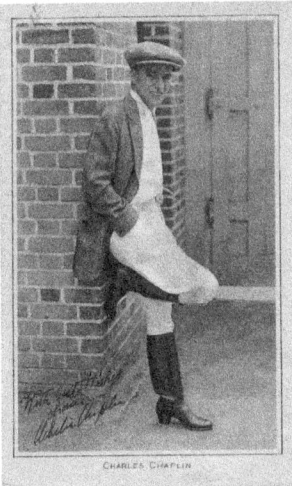

LEFT: Chaplin out of costume after having gone riding with Douglas Fairbanks, 1922. Photograph by Douglas Fairbanks. Courtesy of Douglas Fairbanks Jr. RIGHT: Chaplin's Tramp as seen in his Academy Awardwinning film *The Circus* (1928). Image courtesy of Roy Export SAS, Association Chaplin and Bubbles Inc.© ®Roy Export Co. Inc., All Rights Reserved

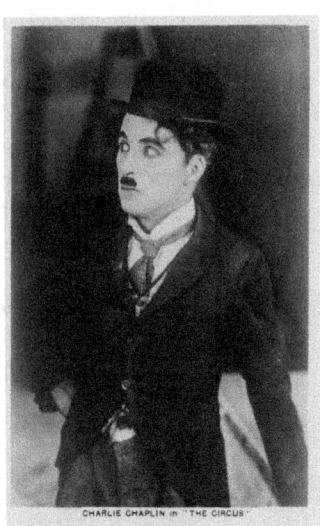

What was that about truth and humor?

Humor is indeed rooted in truth and it doesn't have to be empirical. Hicks' mother Mary, who was in true awe (her exact words) of her son on stage when she *first* saw him, said, "Truth doesn't go away. It is ever lasting. That's what Bill was talking about. Those things don't go away."

Another huge influence to Bill Hicks was Mark Twain and his many masterpieces. (Some believe that Twain is the "the first stand up comedian.")

Hicks repeatedly claimed, throughout his life, and to his friend David Johndrow, that *Huckleberry Finn* (1885) was his favorite book. (Ernest Hemingway believed that "all American literature came out of *Huckleberry Finn*.") One close friend believes the point in the novel where Huck decides to help Jim "exemplifies Bill's whole attitude and was possibly a catalyst in his thinking."[21] Hicks also cottoned to Twain's posthumously published *Letters From the Earth: Uncensored Writings*. His friends felt Bill cackled with joy when reading aloud Twain's hilarious skewering of humanity and religion. Friends received phone calls from the excited comedian who just had to share with his best friend the sheer delight Hicks found in Mark Twain's words. Dwight Slade remembers that "the essential element to Bill was hearing the trains at night go through Houston. We'd think about jumping a train and go to LA to be comedians. That very American element like *Huckleberry Finn*. It cannot be ignored when discussing Bill Hicks' personality. A freedom. An adventurousness."[22] At the end of his life, he owned few possessions. He gave away what little he had and in the final six months of his life, Hicks was a true nomad. Such enhanced his already cosmic consciousness. The road, finite before him, became the most impassioned version in his third act. When asked where he lived, he responded, "I'm residing nowhere. I live here right in these clothes. Send your mail addressed to 'Bill's jeans' care of me." He had no formal home in the final few months of his life.[23]

A preacher. A truth-teller. He was a man who began slaying audiences as a boy of thirteen who was a not old enough to drink in the clubs he started sneaking out at night to perform at. By the time he was fifteen, he was headlining at the Comedy Annex in his hometown of Houston, Texas. Lines of paying customers, who'd spend a minimum of thirty dollars per night, waited in the rain to watch a sixteen year old and be railed at with his cutting edge ideas about life, death, sex, drugs and rock'n roll — *we* state glibly. There was nothing glib about Bill Hicks.

---

[21] Author personal research, email correspondence w/Anonymous, 3 December 2016.

[22] Dwight Slade remembers the Twain connection at 25:08 in Disc 2, Extended Interviews of the AMERICAN documentary

[23] October, 1993, Austin TX Public Access TV "CapZeyz ."

His spiritual center as a seeker of cosmic (if not galactic) "truth" was his anchor as his delivery and venue changed and developed. David Johndrow agreed (that): "Bill was a very spiritually driven person. To miss that is not to 'get' him." In his final two weeks on Earth, Hicks took a vow of complete silence. Only someone spiritually "committed" does this. He was mindful and artful, which is rooted in ephemeral and pragmatic, focused passion; direct sunlight as a person. That is the eighteen-year-old who showed up at The Comedy Store in LA with just a briefcase of clothing, and jokes written on paper. He told the afternoon doorman, "My name is Bill Hicks. I'm here to be a comedian."

Within six months of moving to California, Hicks' name was written in neon as a regular and top dog at The Comedy Store[24] in Los Angeles. While Hicks hated LA as the paradigm of insincerity[25] The Comedy Store also sported names like Robin Williams, and Richard Pryor. Both considered true geniuses, like Hicks' inspiration, Charlie Chaplin. Hicks rarely sought work. He built his act, and the audience discovered him. One journalist described him as being in such demand that he could choose where he worked. His brand of socially aware skewering of sacred cows was a zaniness audiences received psychic relief from. They still do.

Genius. Truth. Humor—what are we *really* discussing? It lies beneath titles. It is invisible, but knowable. One word rests while also sneaking about in the pond of our inquiry. You can't see it, but these clowns make you feel it. Some people call it "soul."

Soul is seen on stage only if an audience can spot it. The soul of many artists is their method. These are actions not always outwardly perceived. To me, part of Hicks' genius was his

---

24 One night at The Comedy Store, in Los Angeles, Bill Hicks and Dwight Slade witnessed an impromptu performance by Richard Pryor and Robins Williams. Circa 1978, Slade remembers they were so close to the master comedians; they seemed to be doing the show for the new young comedians themselves! See: AMERICAN: *The Bill Hicks Story*/Extras/Extended Interviews/Dwight Slade.

25 Old joke: "When you want to tell someone to go fuck themselves in New York, that's what you say. But in LA, they say, 'Let's do lunch' — means the same thing."

constant analysis of what he did. You cannot be Bill Hicks without a great amount of soul; or, earthly desire for transcendence. His was a realization of a greater physical and spiritual reality, which provided fodder for his material world angst. He was monk-like in that he cared little for possessions, constantly sharing and giving away meaningful books, he revered as sacred objects. If John D. Rockefeller was correct when he espoused that "knowledge was power" then Hicks' insatiable bibliomania was the center of his far-reaching, willful, poetic thrust.

It went beyond the material political party with him; that was the hard part for others to see. Labels born of racism infuriated him for the small thinking by minds wasted by such "small thoughts."[26] Yet, his anger was applauded on stage when he imitated one beating on another for their lifestyle. Hicks performance was "dangerous" because it challenged you like a high diving board. Do you have the guts to climb up there and jump off believing it'll work out? Obviously to Bill, this was what performance was all about—going to a new level.

His performance at its best was a charming, jousting paradox on the move and it is fascinating to watch.

My interest with this comet-like talent comes in the aftermath of the personal tsunami he waged on our planet. No, this is not "over-amplification." It is hard for people who have never seen a genuinely break-through comedian or artist of any kind, and to realize it immediately. We are stunned by a new truth. As the name "Houdini" was promoted relentlessly after his death to mean: "magic, escape and the impossible," then Bill Hicks has come to define using "humor to spotlight truth."

A veritable cottage industry profiting the Hicks' family and various producers has sprung up on the Internet offering T-shirts, posters, books, clothing, CD's, and the award-winning, spot-on

---

[26] The sixth astronaut to walk on the moon, Dr. Edgar Mitchell stated that he felt that space itself had a conscious mind. In addition, he told an audience in New Jersey that when the first spaceman arrives on a planet that is not our own, he will *not* say, "Hey, I'm from New York. He'll say, 'I'm from Earth.'" Hicks spoke of humans as One in this vein.

documentary *American: The Bill Hicks Story* (made in England, 2009). Bill Hicks is bigger now (read: "more popular") than he was when he was alive. He is somewhat similar in this phenomenon with his idol Chaplin whose estate grounds and family have brought *Chaplin's World* as a tourist and pilgrim destination in Corsier-sur-Vevey, Switzerland.[27]

It seems that the Europeans have a better view of the truth these two wondrous spirits produced during their lifetimes, because they look with historical hindsight and with geographic distance at the land called "America." Older countries such as India and China are still scratching their heads as to the adolescent behavior of the great USA. Having said that, the commerce created by the American engine joins the great economies of history, no doubt. But, Bill asks, "at what price?"

America tried to kill Charlie Chaplin in 1952. But, Chaplin outwitted his pursuers. America might have killed Bill Hicks. Dying of pancreatic cancer at age thirty-two, the gattling gun that was Hicks' mind was only matched by his spryness and brilliant powers of scrambling while on a football field or the constant refinement of his comedic messages. This was a man who charted his own course, and had the balls to stick to his goal. He was a physically powerful individual his close friend Dwight Slade remembers. Bill Hicks was an intelligent lead-by-example individualist who doesn't accept the diluted Bill of Human Rights masked as law in a Fundamentalist Christian American government. He may be dead, but his message still burns as brightly as magnesium. The Hicks invisible army isn't going anywhere soon. Totalitarianism meets a formidable foe in the man who signed off on phone messages as "Willy." Hicks's open-mindedness concerning the War on Drugs is revealing. It isn't empty hippie logic, it's facts expressed by one involved. It is common sense in short supply in 2017. Hicks shows us that can change with clarity, and a hard good humored look at ourselves.

Both Chaplin and Hicks came of age—as artists—during their youth. While Chaplin fueled the birth of the modern film business, among many other achievements; Hicks'

---

[27] See: www.chaplinsworld.com. Opened April 17, 2016.

accomplishments are too early to gauge the success of historically. In 2016, Charlie Chaplin turned 127. Bill Hicks has been dead for twenty-three years and he'd be the first to say that all comparisons are odious. Though he might phrase it in his Southern preacher voice, laced with animal hypocrisy: *"Now, dontcha go tellin' uthahs that I'm some sort of white light spirit a' happiness*—(now screaming at the top of his lungs)—*I'm a little dark fuckin' poet tonight just plowin' through this crap one more time..."* But then, I'm paraphrasing—badly.

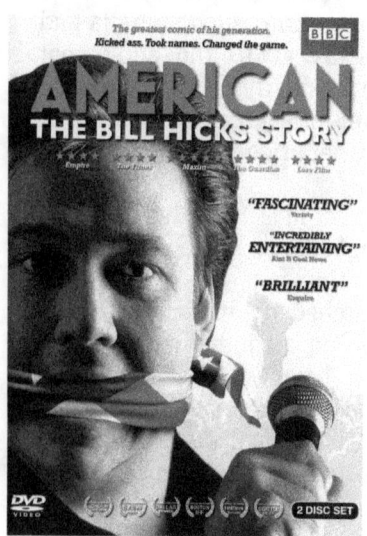 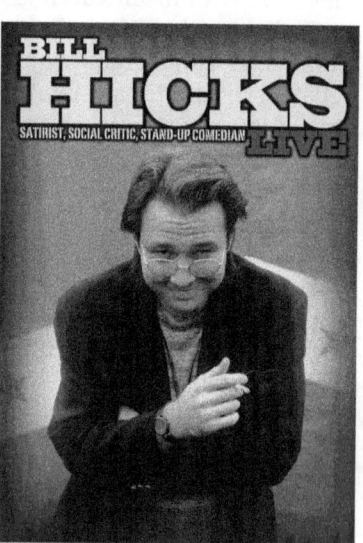

Hicks is a product of the same generation as this writer. He states at the beginning of his fourth and final filmed special titled *Revelations*: "When I was born I was told you could be anything you wanted. A doctor, lawyer, policeman, fireman and something new called an astronaut." In that final artistic incarnation, he entered as the cowboy poet; the scourge of evil, champion of truth, love and transcendent thought to evolve consciousness. The cowboy poet in a sharp black Stetson. In short: a hero.

On stage he joked when appearing in front of two thousand people, *"You're in the right place — It's Bill."* Off stage, he shyly admitted to Charles Brand (producer, *Revelations*), "I can't ride a horse." Nevertheless, you don't need to be able to ride to be a badass. Along with the Lone Ranger, Zorro and Jim West, Wild Bill Hicks' weapon is timeless truth. It aids daily navigation to peace and personal success. The bad guys may have the bullhorn of the mass media, sure. And, Hicks' body may be pushing up roses in Westchester or Austin—yes. Though, what Bill started ain't over yet. Not by a mile or, ten miles. And, here's the best news you've had all day: Unlike Zorro & Co. mentioned previously, Bill Hicks was real. He walked, talked, and provided laughter in the name of peace. Put that in your pipe and smoke it.

BILL HICKS — 1974

Bill Hicks became a comedian shortly after his thirteenth birthday in 1974. On my fourteenth birthday, that same month in that year, I concluded[28] seven years study and research into the Art of Magic. Like Hicks, at an early age, I went pro. I stepped on stage two thousand miles north of where a baby was crying in Texas just thirteen years before. The same month and year Bill Hicks became a comedian, I became a magician.

I offer an autobiographical measuring stick because I understand the adolescent jump into professional performance, rivalry, and failure. Failure on stage meant dire depression. Exhilaration by an adolescent entertaining a room full of skeptical adults is also rarified knowledge, possessed by we who have had this experience. [29]

---

[28] From 1968 to 1974 I read everything on magic in the Ossining, Tarrytown, Briarcliff and Pleasantville, NY libraries concerning magic. After that I decided to try it out on stage.

[29] When I was seventeen, a dramatics professor at Carnegie-Mellon University, told me after my performance for her private party, "Why are you here as a student? You should be teaching us!" She wasn't kidding.

Brander Matthews,[30] tells us: "The magician is a comedian playing the role of a magician." I have wandered for over fifty years in that one sentence. I understand this illusionist who weaved ideas and concepts that were radical, scatological and obscene to some, as I show an audience something right in front of their faces, and they still do not see what I am doing. There is truth to humor and illusion. Humor, exists positively, because, like illusion, there is something hidden. In comedy it is a punch line. In magic, it is a revelation that something unusual has occurred. Success for both depends on not being seen until their arrival. Such is the injection of surprise and genuine mystery as entertainment. Hicks studied this.

Calling Bill Hicks an illusionist is like calling Albert Einstein a math teacher. True—but inappropriate, essentially. Yet, understanding the timing and surprise of a Hicks punch line or performance is to seek the understanding of misdirection, aggressive story-telling and theatrical cadence. If Bob Dylan joked as a younger famous man that he was a "song and dance man," then Bill Hicks equally might have called himself a "dancing poet." A seemingly free-associating poet on the run with a microphone and the energy to spin heads—that's Bill Hicks. Partially.

As a true artist he did not care about being popular, wealthy or getting on TV. Yet, somewhere in his being he also did want those things. Material success took a backseat to a message he was born to give. His material success provided the avenue for his messages to be heard.

He related in interviews later in life that he was born "awake" and that from a very early age he was able to suss-out The Truth in most topics; particularly those that were divisive.

The Hicks approach was in full battle when he approached an audience in San Francisco half way through his forty-five minute set with the words, "Why don't we lighten things up and talk

---

[30] See: Matthews, Brander (former Dean of the Columbia School of Drama), *A Book About The Theatre*, 1911. *The Method of Modern Magic*, p. 256 "He is a conjurer and comedian at the same time."

about abortion? You know...Let's talk about child killing and see if we can't get some chuckles rippling through the room here."

It was his intellectual and spiritual gift from a very early age to realize the relationship between truth and entertainment. If lines were crossed, it would be in the name of equally stated opposing sides. Such as his story about his friends opinions regarding Pro Lifers (anti-abortionists) as "annoying idiots, and the others see Pro Lifers as evil fucks. How are we going to come to a consensus? Brothers, sisters! Can we not come together and just refer to them as 'annoying idiot evil fucks?' I beseech you!"

A parlor game has grown among his fans to try to find a topic Bill Hicks did NOT address. He was an all-encompassing, intelligent voice of reason hidden within a loud, cocky-confident persona that was sexy and forthright. He was tall, handsome and had a sweet face. For a time, he only wore black, and made audiences howl when stating, *"chicks dig the bad boy."* His song titled "Chicks Dig Jerks" on his second album (*Relentless*) also gives an inkling of how historically minded he was, while always making a point with humor. It reminds one of the Manchurian psychologist Dr. Yen Lo telling his Russian counterpart when "building" a perfect assassin Raymond Shaw, in Richard Condon's *The Manchurian Candidate*: "Always with a little humor comrade Zilkov, always with a touch of humor makes things go down far more exceptionally."

LETTERMAN CENSORS BILL HICKS

It was Jay Leno who characterized Hicks as the guy in his comedy class who "told me to fuck off and then walked out slamming the door." Leno said, "those people who walk out, those are usually the best comedians." Leno had brought Hicks to the attention of the show on NBC who booked him eleven times (apparently more than any other comedian) before completely caning his entire fully taped twelfth appearance (for no stated reason at the time) after his material had been approved by NBC "Standards and Practices." (In other words, lawyers who protect the advertisers.) "Protect" is used as in "protect their messages and their interests." You don't book a comedian who bashes a product that is paying huge cash to be included in the overall parade of TV entertainment on *Late Night With David Letterman*. In response, Hicks wrote a thirty-page-plus letter to John Lahr of *The New Yorker*, and also spoke on Austin (TX) Public Access TV about how his relationship with David Letterman was "an abusive relationship—they keep fucking me and I keep coming back for more." [31]

In retrospect, now that the episode has been aired, we can see that Hicks made a joke about Pro Life proponents and suggested that if they were so committed to their cause, they should picket and block the entry to graveyards. Apparently, the following Monday after Hicks' canceled Friday night appearance, *Late Night With David Letterman* included a commercial for, "Pro Life." Letterman was the perfect corporate suck up who did not want to let Bill Hicks bite the hand that fed NBC Advertising such huge barrels of cash. It was part of those barrels' contents that has helped David Letterman purchase a fleet of vintage cars. (An odd similarity to his rival for *The Tonight Show* and the heir to Johnny Carson — the man who did succeed, Jay Leno. The notation is important; not a lot of originality going on by the man who wanted Carson's job. Letterman simply copied the interests of the man who *did get* Carson's throne; the job *Letterman* wanted.)

You want to be an artist and tell the truth? Stay off American television. That is a medium for "suckers of Satan's cock" Hicks was fond of saying. The sounds of his act in this regard have created sleeplessness in many a viewer. He spoke of those who played records backwards and who claimed to hear Satan's voice in that backward play. Hicks commented, "Hey dude, if you are trying to ruin my stereo and play my records backwards, then *you are* Satan!" The laughter cut both ways—believers of inane gossip (and false news) and those of us who deal in fact-driven reality.

In the set (now available on YouTube.com showing David Letterman apologizing to Bill Hicks' mother twelve years after

---

[31] From: CapZeyeZ TV on Austin Public Access, October 24, 1993. Broadcast live at 1:30am. See: YouTube.com

her son's death) Hicks' material was not only approved by the segment producer Robert Morton (aka "Morty"), but by the so-called "censor." It was Letterman himself who canned (censored by deleting) Hicks' appearance. At the time, this cancelation was devastating to the thirty-one year old comedian. Hicks later stated that the censoring of him was a "good thing" because it focused his energies on who he really was, what he was doing, and most importantly, defining his audience. Once cut, he never appeared again because he died roughly four months later. Letterman called the cancelation and death of the young comedian "strange and eerie." That's a convenient aptitude for a man admiring the guts he never had. Such "admiration" showed itself boldly when Letterman and NBC-TV declined to offer a tape of the canceled Hicks performance to the documentary *Outlaw Comic: the Censoring of Bill Hicks* (2003).

By deciding to apologize to Mary Hicks for the "indiscretion" of a canceled live and taped appearance,[ii] Letterman was cashing in on the cult sentiment. While apologizing, Letterman was ham-fisted at best. Quoted by John Lahr in *The New Yorker*, [32]Letterman stated the cancelation (of Hicks' appearance) was "an error of judgment on my part, just a mistake ... born of insecurity more than anything else."

If Letterman had admitted his culpability in the cancelation of Hicks' set, then perhaps he might have been showing true contrition. Instead, he was just taking up airtime with his lame attempt—*twelve years* later!—and jumping on the Hicks bandwagon once more.

David Letterman is not a bonafide superstar that could do anything like Johnny Carson. Actually David Letterman is the biggest Johnny Carson-wannabe that ever lived. Letterman admitted as much over the years. In other words, David Letterman was perfect for American TV. Bill Hicks, given the chance, could have been the end of American TV! Hicks said, "Remember, USA, USA, United States of Advertising." Hicks railed at the insensitivity and contempt network TV had for the audience, particularly the Mid-West where Letterman was from.

---

[32] See Lahr, See: *Bill Hicks, David Letterman and Me*, The New Yorker, April 5, 2011

The hardball of backstage TV worries wrought the beheading of the best comedian to ever play the Letterman show in many people's opinion. David Letterman, figuratively, had the ball, and then dropped it. Exactly as Hicks' performance edict stated: because of fear; without embracing love as one's core. Letterman and his producer Robert Morton claimed they: "loved Bill." But, their actions indicated that they feared him. It cannot be stated more clearly.

Heady stuff? Welcome to the world Bill Hicks not only lived in, but also, exposed, and continues to expose. Hicks was a sword and shield without self-worship that defended against evil with enlightenment, or the pursuit thereof.

Maybe Letterman was confused by Bill Hicks? Because, Hicks actually had something to say that was important; and offered his message(s) by portraying a host of characters in insane or hilarious situations. While comedy may have seemed to be the message, Bill Hicks also was staunch in his belief that the art of the stand up could also shake things up (politically) in an entertaining manner. In his case, the comedian was inseparable from his message. Whatever wrought the cancelation of Hicks' last appearance on *Late Night With David Letterman* it oddly adds to Hicks' puzzling shamanistic journey.[33]

Bill Hicks has now become a worldwide cult icon.

In 2017, David Letterman is worth over three hundred million dollars and makes headlines for growing a beard.

As Bill Hicks said, "Shall I walk you through it again?"[34]

———

From a portrait of those who knew him, he created fervent hope in friends and viewers to a degree. If his message was "counter to the culture" of his time, or the government's agenda, then his

———

[33] See: *Love All The People*, Hicks describes himself as a shaman on page 245 "I am a Shaman come in the guise of a comic."

[34] See: Bill Hicks Live at The Vic Theatre, Chicago, HBO's One Night Stand.

message was indeed based in love and celebration of diversity. He showed us all who we are with an equal yardstick. While he may have offered that those in the advertising industry kill themselves to save their souls *("Because you spew evil garbage that is killing anything good in this world, so kill yourselves")*, his message really was firmly grounded in a personal spirituality and hope that common love would prevail.

Bill Hicks was a loud and precise vacuum cleaner that was devoted to expose hypocrisy, double-standards and blatant falsehoods. Once clean of these philosophical boils perhaps common love and light might prevail. It's a nice thought. Could the evolution of that thought bring that reality? Only time will tell. But, I believe, the once upon a time "outlaw comedian Wild Bill Hicks" moved that concept along nicely (in his stage career, and personal "campaign") to court and experience planetary harmony. The trillions of dollars spent *not* solving problems is a paradigm that pervades almost every aspect of American culture including: law, medicine, finance, and of course, politics. Hicks' misanthropic humanism attacked each area squarely.

After a minute or two of message, delivered in a constant tone, he would perk up, "Hey, don't worry, there's some dick jokes coming."

> *"Don't worry ma'am, you see the way it works is that I do forty-five minutes of editorializing, and then we all pull our chutes together and float down to dick joke island — the heavenly world of dick jokes aplenty."*
> —Bill Hicks, from DANGEROUS.

He delivered comedy and tragedy, sometimes just not in that order. His was refined sweet and salt. It was thrilling to watch his mind at work. Watching a man take chances on stage is akin to watching the high wire walker take each step. It is dangerous territory skillfully negotiated. Audiences may have been surprised by what Bill Hicks said, but they cheered at the end of his performance because he spoke from his heart. There is nobility in one standing up for beliefs. It is deeply human, if not central to life, outside of basic survival. His first two albums define this special artist. *Dangerous* has a cover that depicts Hicks in a smoky room, standing alone, microphone in hand. It is very dark. The next, *Relentless*, offers a portrait of Hicks standing alone in a whited out snowy land before a lone microphone. It is hilarious, pre-apocalyptic and very funny.

If Bill Hicks was a creature of excess, then he applied this to his comedy workmanship to create greater showmanship; constantly using a finer grain of sand paper to attack and praise his art.[35]

Hicks was once part of a marketing package by the Houston Comedy Annex. They sought to book him with five other comedians for a night's entertainment. Their group title, "the outlaw comedians." Hicks' young death perfectly cements his canonization for the "live fast, die young and have a good looking corpse" school of cool. The outlaws were a tight knit bunch who deserve a great deal of study when looking at the short life of Bill Hicks.[36] Being located in Houston Texas, "the outlaws" were a naughty crew (on stage and off stage party habits). But, they delivered a community and brought a teen into adulthood to be a first class comedian.

In death, Bill Hicks has grown into a truly legendary comic outlaw. He shocked because he said what others were thinking. But, he had the courage of his convictions to say what he thought never yielding to hecklers, interlopers, editors or critics. He constantly wondered why people were afraid of his humor. Throughout much of his life he felt alienated and alone. His was a solitary mission. Though, he once confided to a friend that the reason he did what he did, and said what he said, was so *others* would not feel so alone. [37]

He expressed this concern in another way as well. He, like a few other comedians, was an excessive long distance caller to friends all over the world. No matter what time of day it was anywhere in the world "Willy" called and left a message to a seeming baseball roster of best pals. When living in New York's East

---

[35] Hicks considered his art gift to the Great Giver, or his personal God. There was something salutary, he felt, about displaying one's art, and presenting it as best as one could.

[36] See Coda, The Outlaws.

[37] See: True, Cynthia. *American Scream*, Pan Books, 2002, p. 186.

Village in the 1980's, Bill used to stuff his pockets full of dollar bills and many quarters to offer to the "bum gauntlet" he felt he had to pass through when he left his apartment. He speaks about this on *Dangerous* when addressing the failure of social programs by the current administration (1989).

Mindfully artful? He used answering machines as substitute audiences for his quick quips, hilarious diatribes and confessional intimations. Bill was also naturally lonely out on the road. Another small stage with a lone microphone, a brick wall, and some goofy club name like "Uncle Henry's Comedy Couch" becomes old after a few weeks, much less Hicks' rampaging, barnstorming clubs three hundred nights a year. (He also dealt with canceled flights, inept hoteliers, housekeepers disregarding *Do Not Disturb* signs, and other maladies of modernity. He embraced it all. His angst over modernity became the granule of sand in the oyster that makes a pearl.)

Bill Hicks stands for the critical inspection of the truth. In 2017 we need his guidance more than ever. In a weird way, it turns out that Bill Hicks was a prophet. Friends of his only shake their heads and smile, "what would Bill have made of the Internet, email and smart phones, social media and the current political scene!" Then the laughs begin. There is even a book titled *What Would Bill Hicks Say?* This book was published to support Bill's love of animals and the Foundation created in his name for his passionate cause.

————

Richard Jeni (1957—2007) was a comedian of Hicks' era, and knew him. Richard Jeni married the sister of a friend of mine and I'd hear of his tours, triumphs and failures every now and then. Richard Jeni speaks on the short *It's Just a Ride* documentary about Bill Hicks. His final summation was this: "When you watched Bill work, that is, as another comedian occupying the same time and space as this guy. You began to ask yourself questions. He really provoked. And then you started to feel, 'you know, I really ought to be doing more stuff like that'."[38]

Jeni meant, "More stuff like Bill Hicks was doing." In other words, Hicks made other comedians (who cared about their craft) not necessarily jealous, but rather "aware" that there was another way of approaching stand-up comedy that was also socially relevant. Richard Jeni chose his own socially relevant end: he shot himself in the head and died at age fifty.

———————

Bill Hicks was the definition of a man who cared. Paul Daniels once said to me that those who care "are screwed." What Daniels was saying was humorous. (He was making a joke rooted in truth.) Daniels was saying there was more work to be done if one cared about what they were doing. Hicks cared most of the time, except when he was drinking alcohol to excess. He was feted by women strangers who fed him booze and cocaine and then sat back to see what would come out of his mouth on stage while under the influence. Hicks quit drinking and drugging for the greater part of his life, but often joked that he had "no boss, was plied day and night by drugs and women," then he'd take a pause and ask, "Hey! How's your job going?" Boom.

His mindfulness was extreme. He took the events of his own life and made them into comic fodder that fed a much larger (perhaps) selfless agenda. His friend Kevin Booth said that when your inner voice matches your outer voice, then that's art. I agree. I'd go further and add a dissection of what those voices ought to, or can, encompass. While it's immaterial what the artist is like personally, it is the artist's message that compels our study and inquiry. To ask "why" Hicks chose the material he did gives clue to who he was in his core. While his words were his

---

[38] See: *It's Just a Ride*, short form documentary made about Bill Hicks shortly after his death. Seen on the DVD *Bill Hicks Live*.

content, the man behind those words was also a man that thought trying to get laid by getting your date drunk was immoral. Not necessarily a choirboy, his center spiritual compass was fueled by his search for enlightenment. Seen in this context, his "bad boy comedian" actually becomes his costume for delivering a message of ... sanity.

Bill was educated in a Sunday school Baptist church and schooled largely in Texas in the 1960's. His first performance was at a Church Camp. He did not attend college. (Though he did attend Los Angeles Community College for three weeks where he learned karate, but dropped out.) However, in 1990, he toured thirty-one cities in the UK in thirty-three days.

He is recorded on a phone call in the Extras on the *American* documentary. He mentions the touring schedule of he and a road manager pulling into a town, doing the show, and often leaving that night, after the gig in the wee hours—a rough tour without a lot of rest. In modern parlance, performers call this a "surgical strike." Hicks' kind voice offers his interviewer a chance to open the show, a lad of nineteen in Oxford, England who is heard to gasp when the offer was made. Hicks knew and understood young people digging his brand of razor-sharp comedy. I believe Bill was a methodic "giver" who was also clever to compartmentalize associations. One close friend remarked that he'd never met another of Bill's close friends until *after* Bill's death.

Bill Hicks' educational cathedral was his stage; weekly in American clubs such as in Possum Ridge, Arkansas, or when filling the sixteen-hundred seat Oxford Theatre where Oscar Wilde once performed. He noted the differences between playing to five hundred screaming fans in Belfast, Ireland. Then, a week later, playing Adolph's Comedy Bunker in Idaho. Even the less intelligent would have had to see the sad contrast. They'd also see something else if they looked hard enough: Hicks' sheer dedication to doing what he did...no matter where. If he wasn't performing for the audience's present heart; he was refining his craft. Musicians call it "wood shedding." Magicians call it, "Chasing the dream." Both know it means "doing what you were born to do, and having the conviction to see it through." The essential Hicks: all or nothing.

It seems to have been written in stone with him, throughout his life.

———

He began many performances with a call and response to the audience that reminded of an evangelical meeting, broad his silliness was. People thought he was joking when he said, "We gather in the name of the one true god whose name is Love." Actually, he was stating his premise to the vodka-swilling set. Drinking rambunctious audiences (largely in America) were unaware of the penetrating steamship that was about to be driven into their consciousness.

When you are a boy who is either abandoned as a youth, and placed in the situation of having to attain adulthood immediately because death is near; or a dreamer that sets out to set the world on fire with a message, the compass bearings may differ, but the rudder is the same. Passion is that rudder, at the center of an artist's being. Picasso once stated that were he bound, and displaced in a cell, he'd still paint by putting his saliva on the walls with his tongue.

Hicks was absolutely certain from the moment he decided to be a stand up comedian, that come Heaven or Hell, he was going to do it his way. From the first jokes he wrote at age thirteen, to the last words he spoke on stage at Igby's at age thirty-two, Hicks was a literary comedian who sounded as if he was making it up as he went along. (Sometimes that was in fact what was happening on stage. But the truth is, says his friend Andy Huggins, "Bill spent a lot of time writing, refining, try it out and then writing some more." To critic John Lahr, Hicks maintained that he "connected everything on stage" and wrote it as he went along.[39])

Hicks may have been exercising a bit of whimsical misdirection to an admiring fan, Lahr and Lahr's son age sixteen who initially

---

[39] See: Lahr, John, *The Goat Boy Rises*, The New Yorker, Nov. 1, 1993, "Hicks uses the stage time to write his material in front of an audience. 'I do it all onstage, all of it,' he said." Lahr wrote, "Hicks, through laughter, makes unacceptable ideas irresistible."

introduced the father to Hicks. Shortly thereafter the father wrote an extensive piece that was sidelined for months until Hicks was canceled in his final appearance on Letterman. That gave the Hicks profile a healthy currency. But, the myth of "the great Bill Hicks" and the truth of the comedy workman, are hard, if not impossible to separate. He was his product. He was his message. He was his own hypocrite; eating the products he crucified. "Hi, I'm Bill Hicks and I'm an American which you can tell by my lack of class. And I'm proud to represent it." Sometimes the great ones provide a paradox deep in truth; exercised by rampant soul grinning at lesser minds staring, as Bill said, "Like a dog whose been shown a card trick." His attempt to quit cigarette smoking was partially fueled by his dislike of Senator Jesse Helms (North Carolina) and his attachment to "big tobacco." When he informed audiences of his decision to quit smoking, the audience screamed "no!" He replied, "Hey this is not Dylan going electric. Come on!"

When stricken with pancreatic cancer at age thirty-one, he became even more relentless and unflinching. Because, as Bob Dylan wrote, "When you have nothing, you have nothing to lose." Cancer did not stop Bill Hicks—it pushed him to create more in the limited time he had.[40] No one could ever accuse this artist of being impure. He was an honest soul who never deviated from his self-imposed mission. (He turned down all commercial endorsement offers saying assuredly, "I am not a salesman.") We'll leave that mission for you to discover and analyze.

For this exceptional comedian-satirist, his passion was the truth; what was real. He made his point so starkly clear that the surprise of his intonation was hilarious. As a dancer portraying a "trickster god" he pranced about the stage with an airiness that looked and felt as if he were floating. Like his hero Chaplin, he made people scream with laugher with an exaggerated face. Then the teen scrambler from his high school football field grew into a swirling, twirling comedic preacher; a poet seeker speaker. Belly laughs abounded from a verbal set up with a physical comedy punch line such as the silent "thank you" by a Middle

---

[40] In the last months of his life Bill Hicks recorded material for two albums. Nearly a dozen albums have been posthumously released.

Eastern man receiving a banana shot down his throat by "smart war technology." Waving to an invisible airplane, Hicks as the recipient of the banana, brought down the house.

Bill Hicks was electric on stage fueled by the charisma of his beliefs; the passion of his personal search for "greater truths." Greater truths? Yes — looking beyond your simple life into concepts such as the "greater good," karmic offenses and efforts at changing social order; based on love, as opposed to fear. Misrepresented in some articles as an "atheist comedian" some missed the point that challenging organized religion doesn't make one an atheist. Instead, Bill Hicks was a very spiritual cat. (Dressing in black, smoking cigarettes on stage and using profanity are not actions anathema to raw spirituality.)[41] He politely debated English church officials who were outraged at his act in Britain. Letters he received were adroitly and answered honestly without anger.

On stage, he could dance, he could move, he was sexual abandon let loose. Everyone liked it. And then, replicating a hallucinogenic adventure with friends, audiences doubled over in laughter when he said, "So you guys can use your legs huh?" His graceful physical actions set up contrast to the stationary-delivered line about lack of mobility. Brilliant. Artful. Mindful. A deeper entertainment.

He knew the pictures he could make with one face or with graceful motion—inspired predominantly by Chaplin—was certainly one of his goals of performance. If he could get good laughs without saying a word, Bill Hicks was possessed to learn how. Some of his funniest moments are when he extends his lower lip to show sarcastic contrition for having either had a "good time on drugs" or when advising other hallucinating members of his car pool to "Be cool."

---

[41] In fact, if agreeing with Rogan Taylor's broad hypothesis that shamanism became show business, Hicks' performance becomes a spot on paradigm of such thinking. See: *The Death and Resurrection Show*, Anthony Blond publishers, London, 1985. Hicks' whole life was shamanism in three acts to the dedicated researcher

The beginning of the *Sane Man* set of performances captured on tape and the opening to *One Night Stand* are remarkably similar, the concept having been born with his crew, and later appropriated by HBO for the good idea it was. They open each show with a docile ode to silent film comedy, Bill being yanked into the stage door entrance in *One Night Stand*. The opening tracking shot in black and white done via bicycle, for the indie self-produced *Sane Man* was quickly adopted as sped up black and white overly grainy footage for his *One Night Stand* HBO special.

At the end of some of his larger stage shows[42] Hicks was dramatically assassinated. Gunshots ripped out of the sound system and the comedian fell over. He slumped motionless as if he were JFK in the Zapruder film. The comparisons were inspired—he injected everything he could into his performance to make an impression, never with sappy gimmickry.

Hicks was not afraid of publically uncovering — or discovering — pernicious secrets of criminality and taking such information to the public. As long as he spoke the truth in well-delivered, hilarious comedic repartee, few challenged his point of view. (When he was heckled, he fought to the death against ignorance —and the laziness of drunks with nothing important to add. As he exposed hypocrisy and injustice, he was entrenched on stage almost as if a warrior on the battlefield. He did not pick fights per se. He defended his fight against what he felt unjust or hypocritical.) He once lambasted a drunken woman in Chicago who offered loudly, "You suck!" Hicks screamed, after hearing her shrill interruptions one too many times: "Get her out. Get out! Get the fuck out you screaming cunt. Get the fuck out. I have feelings too." The tension over an impending brawl was the intense drama a Hicks performance could summon. It is not every comic who can entertain with summoning bold truth. It is risky territory. Backstage stories exist on videotape of Hicks and crew darting from thrown bottles once they had the cash for the evening. It was a Louisiana gig where the audience was ready to kill the comedians. We praise this outlaw and band—the drama

---

[42] See: performance at The Vic Theatre, Chicago, for HBO *One Night Stand*; *Just For Laffs Festival*, 1991; and Dominion Theatre, London performance, 1992. All seen on *Bill Hicks Live* DVD, assembled and produced by Ryko.

of their youth is our historic entertainment. Broken bones meant their war was on. Truth be heard—is *outlaw*? Truth is outlaw to audiences that don't recognize it.

In his first taped "TV special" titled *Sane Man* —1989— he's recently gained sobriety, and as many associated with the program remembered, "Bill was on fire with new, original material. He was at the height of his powers."[43] (Sane Man was previously a character created by Hicks in high school, more as a super hero for a comic book than any "meta" representation of himself.)

But, the two-show performances cut into one DVD of these performances is a revelation to his sober "breaking through." Hicks expels his personal devils and shows his comic "awareness" by metamorphosing before the audiences very eyes into a multitude of characters.

It wasn't just good acting. It was impassioned juxtaposition; shamanic, if you really want to get down to it.

Can one who is *not* a shaman perform shamanic acts? If so, then Bill Hicks was that man, not on stage, but off. His on stage characters and voices, rhythms and choices were all of a tea totaling, innocent individual often ignorant of the hardships he later came to know so well. At a very young age, Bill Hicks traveled a road to perfect his craft for one purpose only: to seek, and share actual enlightened thinking. That's hard to swallow, when the man delivering this message is talking about blowing himself on stage. *Boom.*

Some characters lasted the rest of Hicks' career; others vanished after that night's performance. The producer of those taped shows in Austin, had not seen his friend in a while prior to the shows. He stated that while they may not have known exactly what they were doing with some borrowed local TV equipment; the performance defines the great essence of Bill Hicks. I believe that in this *Sane Man* performance, we actually do see the caterpillar emerging from the chrysalis as the butterfly.

---

[43] Personal correspondence with the author, December 2016.

EFFORTLESSNESS-SELFLESSNESS-FEARLESSNESS

But then, you have to know more about this artist than just laugh at one of his shows. *Sane Man*, however, seems to be the match that caught fire. While the boy comedian had attained "success" of an audience waiting on line to see him "rule the room" it is this performance (actually two shows cut together) where I appreciate his seeming comic effortlessness (as if he had not written out the words before speaking them), selflessness and above all, his fearlessness in front of an audience and cameras. At the time Hicks was twenty-seven. Kevin Booth worked the sound. David Johndrow operated the cameras. *Sane Man* had a two-man production crew Hicks could implicitly trust to provide the finest representation of his work to date. They were his best friends and theirs was a mutual devotion to deliver for each other. Complementary commitment.

Like Val Kilmer playing Jim Morrison on 16mm film and sending this "audition tape" to Director Oliver Stone who cast him as Jim Morrison in his film *The Doors*, Hicks created *Sane Man*, and HBO bit. Their *One Night Stand* series verily duplicated the lower budget effort by Hicks, Booth and Johndrow. Oh, and just so you know, yes, Bill did get the job playing Bill. Just wanted to make that clear.

"If you can't buy it, and no one will lend it to you—steal it." Those words were used by me and my crew when punching holes in ceilings to make lighting poles fit during college gigs to make the performance more theatrical. When you are young, you do with what you have. *Sane Man* was Hicks exercising these values. Bill knew that commerce, economy, laws and "show biz" news on TV was illusory. This knowledge, while earthbound, is difficult to handle. It is like knowing a secret you wished others shared. Hence Hicks angst.

ONE MAGICAL MOTHERFUCKER

People walked out of a Bill Hicks show enlightened, sometimes angered, but most always thrilled to have heard the news that doesn't appear on TV. (One time after a show several offended Christians broke Hicks' leg. No matter, the crutches became props fueling his comic rage.) He mentioned positive drug stories with LSD because he had tripped with hallucinogenic mushrooms in the safety of a Texas ranch. He sought the consciousness expansion brought forth by ancient meditation and he described his friend's experience with boarding an alien ship, as he did too. His friend Kevin Booth wondered, "How did Bill know what I was thinking?" His friend David Johndrow concluded, "If you look hard enough you will find that this world is one magical motherfucker." [44]

The world is a lot less magical without Bill Hicks.

Now, here's a small quiz: How many times up to this point (only) have I mentioned "Bill Hicks?" (Forget book and video titles.) When you go back and find the answer, think about how this article begins. I daresay that when you begin to weave your own webs of meaning, revelation will occur. (At least that is my fervent hope.) Copy not the example, but use hidden mindfulness (mine and yours) to create your own. If you do this work long enough, you will crash through the threshold of an artfulness that cannot be acquired any other way. You will begin to discover hidden rhythms.

All of a sudden, whether it is a great clown, actor, dancer, painter or comedian, it will be as if a mortal coil will have been shuffled off—pleasantly so. I am sure this revelation occurred for Bill Hicks in his discovery and enjoyment of his heroes, Charlie Chaplin, the Marx Brothers, W.C. Fields and Mark Twain.

---

[44] The quote is from the *American: The Bill Hicks Story* (2009) documentary. Terence McKenna (1946–2000) and his brother Dennis found similar phenomenon while ingesting similar hallucinogens as explained in the book *True Hallucinations* (1993). Bill Hicks was a profound McKenna acolyte having been introduced to McKenna by his friend David Johndrow.

If you choose a path of artful inquiry (not just seeking "what" but also "why"), intellectually, or on foot, your artfulness will be born of mindfulness concerning hidden or overt meaning.

If you seek to impress, educate, entertain or simply communicate, this is the key—a way to create without financial expenditure. Bill Hicks performance is just one profound example of using your head, educating yourself to the building blocks of reality; and then selflessly sharing that understanding with others to evolve thought. Simple solutions to complex problems are the work of those who see the future by imagining it first.

Bill once said that being a comedian was *not* a "cool show business job." For himself, and us, he was a clear seer. In French that amounts to the word "clairvoyant." He said he chased the truth like a hound.

Bill Hicks' life and art is ongoing and pure.

And it has been, since Bill Hicks was born — and then died, *screaming* in America.

The Hicks' family released this statement by their son, written one week before his death on February 26, 1994:

I was born William Melvin Hicks on December 16, 1961 in Valdosta, Georgia. Ugh. Melvin Hicks from Georgia. Yee Har! I already had gotten off to life on the wrong foot. I was always "awake," I guess you'd say. Some part of me clamoring for new insights and new ways to make the world a better place. All of this came out years down the line, in my multitude of creative interests that are the tools I now bring to the Party. Writing, acting, music, comedy. A deep love of literature and books. Thank God for all the artists who've helped me. I'd read these words and off I went – dreaming my own imaginative dreams. Exercising them at will, eventually to form bands, comedy, more bands, movies, anything creative. This is the coin of the realm I use in my words – Vision. On June 16, 1993 I was diagnosed with having "liver cancer that had spread from the pancreas." One of life's weirdest and worst jokes imaginable. I'd been making such progress recently in my attitude, my career and realizing my dreams that it just stood me on my head for a while. "Why me!?" I would cry out, and "Why now!?" Well, I know now there may never be any answers to those particular questions, but maybe in telling a little about myself, we can find some other answers to other questions. That might help our way down our own particular paths, towards realizing my dream of New Hope and New Happiness. Amen. I left in love, in laughter, and in truth and wherever truth, love and laughter abide, I am there in spirit.[45]

[45] Official Bill Hicks website www.billhicks.com, statement, archived 1994, retrieved, 2007. See: *Wikipedia* reference on Bill Hicks. Also see: www.sacredcow.com

SELECT DISCOGRAPHY & SUGGESTED READING:

All widely available on Amazon.com, eBay.com
or your favorite underground shopping sites.
Watch, listen and read daily to maintain sanity.
(Keep that third eye squeegeed.)

Listening:

Dangerous
Relentless
Arizona Bay
Rant in E-Minor
Hicksville! An Introduction to the Genius of Bill Hicks
Bill Hicks—Satirist, Social Critic, Stand Up Comedian
(recorded for in store and radio promotion)
Philosophy: The Best of Bill Hicks
Bill Hicks: Love, Laughter and Truth
Flying Saucer Tour Vol. 1
Shock & Awe: Live at Oxford Playhouse (Invasion Records)
Salvation: Oxford November 11, 1992 (Ryko Dist.)
Tool: Aenima (see: Another Dead Hero)
Marblehead Johnson

Listening & Viewing:

Bill Hicks—The Complete Collection—12 CDs, 6 DVDs, 1 book
Bill Hicks—The Essential Collection—2 CDs, 2 DVDs, 1 download card

Viewing:

Ninja Bachelor Party
Sane Man
One Night Stand
Relentless
Revelations
American: The Bill Hicks Story (documentary)
It's Just a Ride (documentary)
Outlaw Comic: The Censoring of Bill Hicks (documentary)

Chronological Writing:

Grace, Arthur, *COMEDIANS*, Eastman-Kodak Co. & Thomasson-Grant Publishers, US, 1991. While not mentioning Bill Hicks specifically, this book gives an excellent overview of the life of a stand up comedian in the 20th century.

Lahr, John, *The Goat Boy Rises*, The New Yorker, November 1, 1993. (An expanded version appears as a Foreword to *Love All the People*.)

Lieck, Ken, *OVERDUE BILL*, The Austin Chronicle, Austin, Texas, October 4, 1996. p. 30. Cover Story about Bill Hicks and his estate and what happened to the recordings he left behind. Written by an FOB.

True, Cynthia, *American Scream—The Bill Hicks Story*, Pan Books (Macmillan Books, UK), London, 2002.

Outhwaite, Paul, *One Consciousness: An Analysis of Bill Hicks' Comedy*, D.M. Productions, Middlesbrough, England, 3rd revised and expanded edition, 2002.

Hicks, Bill, *Love All The People—The Essential Bill Hicks*, Soft Skull Press, NY, 2004.

Booth, Kevin and Bertin, Michael, *Bill Hicks: Agent of Evolution*, HarperCollinsBooks UK, London, New York, 2005.

Mack, Ben, and Pulkkinen, Kristin, editors, *What Would Bill Hicks Say?*, Soft Skull Press, Inc., Brooklyn, NY, 2006.

Robinson, Ben, *Mindful Artfulness* (Part II: Who They Were: *Bill Hicks 1961—1994*), Paul Romhany publisher, Vancouver, Canada, 2017.

CODA: THE BEGINNING IS THE END

The OUTLAWS
written & sung poolside
by Bill Hicks
Houston, Texas, July 17, 1988
©2010, Arizona Bay Production Co. All Rights Reserved.
from: Bill Hicks—The Complete Collection

There once was this group of guys
Gleam of madness in their eyes
Wanted to make their mark on the world
Outlaws was their name and,
Comedy was their game
Along with trying to meet some girls
There was Shock with his attitude cocky and wise
There was John who was cool with shades on his eyes
Es-quire, hot as a pis—tol
Andy and Riley characters abound
There was Bill dressed in black and livin' downtown
And Eppy with his jack off jokes and crystal suit.

How it all got started I'll never know
It probably came up in a drunken row
Hey, I've got it, someone slurred
"Let's all get together and take the world
We'll need some money and make some girls"
Success and stardom—we de-serve.
No more Paul, no more Shack
Fuck'em a-l-l
We'll meet at Bill's
Tomorrow at Noon, we'll argue til' he wakes
And we'll go for food
Have to decide — whose our leader
Riley thinks he's the one for the job
Eppy thinks Riley is a slob
Shock says "fuck it, let's go eat"
And that's agreed on
Riley wants to eat at the Black Eyed Pea

Shock says he wants Vietnamese
Eppy says wherever Shock goes is the place for him

Andy and Jimmy are broke today
Bill says he'll cover if they'll repay
I guess that means, John says, "We're done workin'"
Where O where did the Outlaws go?
They're out to lunch and they got a show
Looming on the horizon
(Ah) Hicks is asleep and Shock is stoned
Where Eppy went, nobody knows
No one seems to care to find him
As frightening as it seems
Eppy had a dream
By the time we found out it was time to
l e a v e
More than a little bit scary
On a dingy little club in Chicago-land
We were up shit's creek without a fan
Except for one cackling idiot named Barry

A what ever happened to the Outlaw Live
Shock's too busy juggling wives
John thinks Eppy is a putz
For the umpteenth time Jimmy up and quits
Andy'd be happy with a solid shit
Riley has his mind on a ki-butz

Interviewer: **"That's sad."**

BH: **"That's real sad"**

Interviewer: **"Are those tears or sweat?"**

BH: **"Both. Little of both."**

This performance was seemingly impromptu recorded
shortly before Hicks moved from Houston to New York. He
was interviewed after this short song.

BACKWARD/DRAWKCAB

My name is Bill Marx, and I am descended from a long line of laughs. And punch lines. Those laughs were provided by my family of uniquely funny human beings, the Marx Brothers, as well as their comedic colleagues from vaudeville and motion pictures: Burns, Jessel, Benny, Chaplin, Keaton, Fields, etc. The Brothers brought to the world their very own surrealistic view of reality, one that is still as contemporary today as when they first blindsided the world with their marvelous madness at the turn of the 20th century. Their Marx mirthful manifesto has endured the test of time, most probably because their humor is basically derived from exposing all the negative human behavior we have become so accustomed to seeing in others, all the while fighting our very own, desperately trying to keep as dormant as humanly possible. After all, humans will be humans.

The caped heroes of today that really keep us in touch with our questionable behavior and shows us how little our so-called superior species of animal has actually evolved over the years are, ta-tah, the world's comedians and humorists, purveyors of an alternate? sanity in a less than perfect world. They cleverly work their humorous verbal and physical sleight of hand in addressing that which would be normally considered mundane, everyday life occurrences, leading us by the hand down roads all too well traveled and then applying the coup de gras maneuver, that of a totally unexpected ending, certainly a commonality so very much akin to the magician's ultimate purpose of similarly manipulating our minds. Joke setups, whether satirical, social commentary, slapstick or puns intended, lead us off in one direction by temporarily diverting our captive attention until the deliverance of the unsuspecting wallop of its punch line. And for that moment, humor, like magic, transports us away from our reality and into our wonder. Then imagine this! We will laugh and applaud the very thing that makes us realize for a split second how we've just been had! Surprise is the antidote for countering the normal, and we actually love being duped by funny. (Jack Benny—"Funny is funny.") And funny makes us feel so good, because it provides us with a pure path to our own perception of our own truth.

Magicians unload their craft on audiences by creating visual illusions of grandeur. (Chico Marx—"Who are you going to believe, me or your own eyes?") The magician brings his own truth to the party.

This book has blended together the merging talents of our distinguished author-magician, Mr. Robinson, and the unfortunately long-lost until now humoristic brilliance of Bill Hicks, comedian. In looking backward, they both shared the valued history that preceded and prepared them for their life's commitment to and confidence in doing what they loved most, making audiences think.

And if you look even closer, you'll detect a shared sense in each of their uncommon work that they have in common upon being reflected outwardly: that perceptible wonder shining through a little joyous twinkle in their eyes, signifying to us they know something special that we don't.

My own backward contribution to this wondrous book has been an honor bestowed upon me by a man whose unusual and difficult childhood life was dramatically changed when, at an early age, he was first introduced to a magical and comedic Harpo moment in one of my father's movies. From that pivotal blip in his time, young Ben knew his destiny was to be what he has become, a world famous MAGICian. And from the books he has authored including his most recent enthralling trilogy, Mr. Robinson, the magician, has apparently learned throughout his prolific years that, after all, humans will continue to be humans.

—Bill Marx

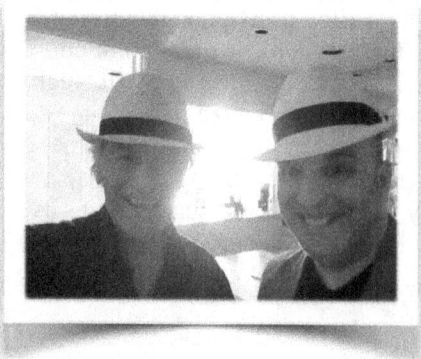

The author and Bill Marx

ODE TO THE OUTLAW COMIC BILL HICKS *

Oswald didn't kill Kennedy, but was murdered same
Declaring the Truth, in the rightful name
Editors of poetic, operatic, misanthropic humanism

Tarnish the shine of morons' consumerism
O' we seek the pitiful Truth

Teach us Bill by tearing off the roof
Hearty laughter is the proof
Each day we desire Hicks' wickedly funny tumult

Outlaw comic Hicks, got the desired result
Upbraiding society he sought to fix (as)
The sharp black hat cowboy, Outlaw Comic "Wild Bill" Hicks
Laughter, jokes, puns—no card tricks (shown to dogs)
Always hilarious, artful, never low
Wahoo! He's here—welcome our comedic hero

Cocksure with each joke — we love his sound
Ordeal, schlemiel, upside-down absurdities abound
Mimicry second-to-none, on solid ground
Identifying illusions amidst the day
Colliding political clowns into the fray

Bill Hicks lives I am sure
I'd bet on it, as he is pure
LSD, sex, laughter and bliss
Look around and you won't miss

Hicksian hilarity heals — undeniably
Illusions of reality popped indubitably
Causation, sensation, failure and reward
Know this Earthlings: move *f o r w a r   d*
Suckers of Satan's cock beware, beaucoup d'affaire

—Ben Robinson

*A/o Sept. 2017, see **www.illusiongenius.com** Writer page link to a special song of this poem.
Secret download code is: BILLHICKS

IN MEMORIAM

Name: William Melvin Hicks (known as "Bill Hicks")
Occupation: Stand-up Philosopher
Employed: US, Canada, Australia, England
Born: Valdosta, Georgia, December 16, 1961
Died: Little Rock, Arkansas, February 26, 1994
Age: 32 years, 2 months, 10 days.
Buried: Leakesville, Mississippi family plot

Whereabouts: "Wherever truth, love and laughter abide,
                    I am there in spirit."

Ongoing: www.billhicks.com   www.sacredcow.com

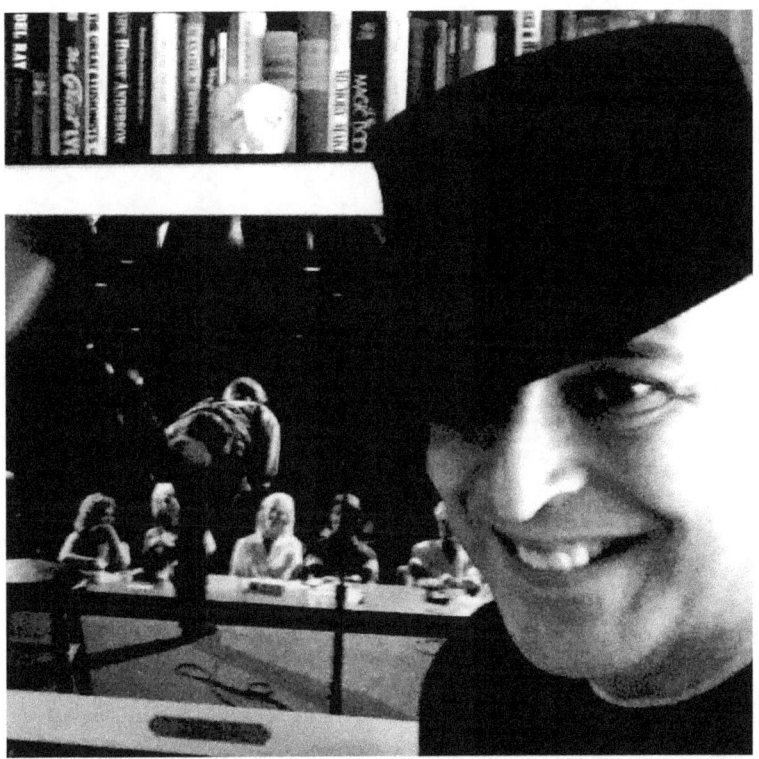

THE AUTHOR

Ben Robinson is a master magician who lives in the center of one of the world's largest cities. He's written twelve books, starred in six one-man shows, and appeared in twenty-two countries for approximately three million people live. For 40-years his life has been dedicated to inspiring wonder, spreading laughter and expanding consciousness for himself and his audience. He and his wife An are owned by an ever-spry parrot named Stubby. Illusiongenius.com.